Coffee with the Pastor

Walking in the Light

I, II, III John

MIKE HILSON

CONTENTS

ACKNOWLEDGMENTS

I want to thank my wife, Tina, who has been my partner in life and in ministry: I love you! To our three boys, Robert, Stephen, and Joshua, thank you for taking this journey of ministry with us and having a great attitude about it along the way. Also, thank you for growing up to be reliable, solid men on whom I can count on and in whom I take great, hopefully godly, pride.

I want to sincerely thank my family at New Life Church for giving me the freedom to grow as a leader and as a follower of Christ.

Most importantly, I want to thank and praise God!

ABOUT THIS BOOK

People sometimes ask why I would take the time to write a book. The answer is really quite simple and two-fold. First of all, I want to be able to speak with my children, my grandchildren, and my great-grandchildren about this wonderful Gospel that I have been given the honor of working for all my life. I want them to see the joy and power of living a life guided and protected by God's word, God's Spirit, and God's commands. In doing so, I hope to establish many generations of my family in the wonderful grace of our Lord.

So I write as a father.

I also write as a pastor.

New Life Wesleyan Church has become a rather large body of believers meeting in multiple services and multiple locations across multiple states. While all of that is a huge praise report and more of a blessing than any of us who work here could have ever hoped for, it creates its own set of challenges. It has become impossible for me to sit down individually with folks in the church like I did once before and have deeper conversations about the power of God's word and how it can be applied in their lives. And so ... this is the reason for a series of books called *Coffee with the Pastor*.

As I write these books, I do so with a great deal of care and caution. They will read, to many people, like a commentary of sorts. However, let me warn you about that thinking. I am not qualified to write commentaries. I am not a theologian. I am not a scholar. I am simply a pastor, and as a pastor it is my job to help as many people as possible to read and better understand the word of God. His word is powerful and life-changing. If you can just get into it and understand what it is saying, you can see the God of Heaven through the blood of Jesus and the power of the Holy Spirit, and that will change your life! Therefore, though this work is bathed in as good as an understanding of theology as I can attain, the goal is not theological. The goal is practical application of life-changing, biblical truth.

That is the purpose of this series of books. That actually is the purpose of my ministry. That actually is the ultimate goal of my life.

So, grab a cup of coffee, understand that I am no scholar, open up your Bible, and let's get you thinking about what God can do in your life!

INTRODUCTION

"That which was from the beginning, which we have heard, which we have seen with our eyes, which we have looked at and our hands have touched—this we proclaim concerning the Word of Life." (1 John 1:1)

I have always loved the book of 1 John. I remember as a teenager reading through this particular book of the Bible. One verse stood out to me: *"My dear children, I write this to you so that you will not sin"* (1 John 2:1). I remember that I was pretty shocked to read this as a teen. I had lived a pretty defeated life up until that point. I was small for my age, a musician, not very attractive, and not at all popular. I also was regularly defeated in my spiritual life. The entire environment of my life had taught me that I was not going to succeed ... at least the way I saw it.

Then there was this scripture.

As unbelievable as it was to me, it was God's word. I knew that God's word was always right and always true. I realized that if God's word said that the Apostle John was writing to me so that I *"will not sin,"* then there was hope for me. I could be more. I could be better. I could succeed in ways that I had not considered possible. And suddenly my whole world looked different. Defeat did not have to be my default setting.

So I tried harder.

I did better.

Then I messed up again ... and I chose to memorize the rest of the verse: *"But if anybody does sin, we have an advocate with the Father—Jesus Christ, the Righteous One"* (1 John 2:1).

Now there was more than hope. There also was grace. Hope that I could be more, and grace when I somehow failed to achieve the goal of being more. That perspective literally changed the way I viewed my life, and my future. In this book, it is my prayer that the Epistles of John will have the same effect on you. You do not have to be defeated. You do not have to be broken. You can truly experience New Life in Christ. You can finally *"walk in the light, as he is in the light"* and *"have fellowship with one another, and the blood of Jesus, his Son, purifies us from all sin."* (1 John 1:7).

WEEK

1

Day 1

"In the beginning was the Word, and the Word was with God, and the Word was God." (John 1:1)

I am starting with a look at the first Epistle (letter) of John by quoting the first verse of the Gospel of John. These are very different books, although they carry very similar themes. I do this to help set the background for what we are about to read. The Apostle John, also known as John the Beloved, is the author of the Gospel of John; the Epistles of I John, II John, III John; and Revelation. As John writes this letter, he is facing a church struggling to define its understanding of whom Jesus is and what His life should mean for us. Many different views on Jesus and who He was were emerging from those who did not walk with Christ or personally encounter Him. These views varied wildly and sometimes led to destructive ends. The Apostles were the ones who knew Jesus, and their viewpoint of Him remained remarkably uniform. Their view was grounded in the knowledge of the man, Jesus, and an experience with that man who also was Christ, Messiah, and Son of God. Therefore, their view of who Jesus was and what Jesus taught did not swing wildly with the given opinions of the day.

The others who wrote and pontificated on their opinions about Jesus did so without the benefit of a relationship with Him, and, just like today, that relationship makes all the difference. These people who taught a view of Christ different from the Apostle's

1

view of Christ, the Apostle John viewed as antichrists. These antichrists were largely Gnostics. Gnostics held the view that Jesus was not really human. They believed that God could not have possibly indwelt a material, physical body. To these people, the material world was evil and all physical things were bad. The only thing that mattered was the internal, spiritual soul. They even went so far as to argue that the world was not created by God, but instead created by some lower angelic force that spun into existence a lower form of being (man), in whom God must then rescue their spiritual souls.

The result of this thinking was really ugly. Gnostics fell into three very real traps that were entirely destructive to their spiritual lives, and if accepted by the Church would have destroyed Christianity. I've defined these three traps below:

1. Heresy

Jesus is the Son of God. He is simultaneously human and God. He is the only one that has ever existed in such a dual state, yet the Gnostics did not believe this duality. To reject Jesus' divinity (His God-ness) is to reject the revelation of God given to us through Jesus. Think about it. If Jesus is not God, then I suppose a human is capable of saving all of humanity. That seems like a stretch! If Jesus is not God, then His statements about being the Son of God make him a liar. It's tough to view Him as a great moral teacher or sufficient sacrifice for our sins if He is ultimately just a liar! Finally, if Jesus is not God, from where does our hope come? These Gnostics would try to adhere to the Old Testament law in order to find a workable "religion" to practice, but even that didn't help their deeply broken theology. In this way, Gnosticism sounds a lot like the legalists of our day with the thinking that you must follow the law without breaking it ... or you are condemned! This gave way to heresy. The problem here is obvious; we just aren't capable of following the law without breaking it. Ever since Moses gave us the law, we have about 4,000 years of evidence to prove that. We need a Savior from God who IS God, and that Savior is Jesus. Jesus is God.

2. Arrogance

The word Gnostic is taken from the Greek root word gnosis. This word means knowledge (Strong 2010, p. 61). What the Gnostics believed was that somehow he (or she) had been given a special knowledge or understanding from God that others were not given. This special knowledge is what brought salvation to the Gnostic. Now think this through. If I am "saved" because of some special insight God has only given me and not you, then I guess I am just better than you! You see the problem here, don't you? Gnosticism really sounds a lot like some of the arrogance we see today in the intellectual elite. They miss the profound wisdom of simple love because they cannot see past the clouded theories of complex law. Jesus is God and He loves everyone!

3. Immorality

According to the Gnostics, the entire physical or material world was evil. This evil could not be broken or mended; therefore, there was no reason to even try. The Gnostic would attempt to follow the law as best as he or she could in order to feed the spirit that was inside. Whenever the law was broken, that was just the brokenness of the flesh that sinned; it was not the enlightened spirit that lived inside of that broken flesh. The spirit held no responsibility for the actions of the flesh. The spirit was simply a victim trapped within the evil flesh. So if my body sinned, that wasn't my fault! That was the fault of the evil material I was trapped in. Wow! Doesn't that sound vaguely familiar? Since there is no responsibility for actions of the physical body, then any experience that somehow allowed the spirit to better experience, understand, or gain knowledge (gnosis) of the world was considered positive, even when it was sinful. This gave way to immorality. The truth is that Jesus is God. He loves everyone and demands righteousness.

It is into this context and culture that the Apostle John writes, and we must keep this in mind as we look into his words. Now let's take a look at 1 John!

Day 2

"That which was from the beginning, which we have heard, which we have seen with our eyes, which we have looked at and our hands have touched—this we proclaim concerning the Word of life. The life appeared; we have seen it and testify to it, and we proclaim to you the eternal life, which was with the Father and has appeared to us." (1 John 1:1-2)

One central theme that we are going to repeatedly run into here in the Apostle John's writing is this: Christianity is not so much a religion as it is a relationship. John often speaks about loving God and others. In the Gospel of John, he calls himself the *"disciple whom Jesus loved"* (John 21:7). A relationship with Jesus is absolutely central to the Apostle John. This relationship makes all the difference, especially in the cultural context that this infant church was facing at the time the Apostle writes.

The Gnostics were running around claiming that Jesus was not really Christ. In fact, they were saying that Jesus was merely a man, 100% human and nothing else. They believed that at Jesus' baptism, the spirit of the Christ came upon him and guided him throughout his ministry. Then on the cross, the spirit of the Christ left him to die as a mere mortal. In other words, they didn't so much believe that Jesus was the Christ, as they believed that Jesus was simply the vessel used by the Christ to accomplish its own spiritual goals. That left them chasing after a spirit of Christ that was ethereal, mystical, foggy, distant and difficult, if not impossible to know or understand at all. That is why their teaching of some special knowledge of the spirit was so powerful. While others listened to them and couldn't make heads or tails out of what they were saying, they seemed smart and sincere. So the thinking was simple: They must know something that I don't! They must be smarter, more spiritual, more connected, and more special than me. And the Gnostic teachers were more than happy to let that belief thrive. It gave them power and position in society. It made them the heroes.

But that isn't what the Gospel is about. Jesus is the Hero! Jesus is the Christ! Jesus is God! It is to that reality that the Apostle John writes. He is seemingly screaming at the top of his lungs:

WE HEARD HIM! WE SAW HIM! WE LOOKED INTENTLY AT HIM! WE TOUCHED HIM WITH OUR OWN HANDS! JESUS REALLY WAS, AND IS, WHO HE SAID HE WAS!

Jesus was no ghost, no fake, no liar, or no possessed individual. Jesus was, IS, the Messiah, the Christ. And that is the point that the Apostle is desperately trying to repeat and drive deep into this infant church.

If you miss this, you miss it all!

His words here are more powerful than they seem on the surface and they hold a great lesson for us about experiencing the reality of Jesus, the Christ.

Hear Christ – *"We have heard"*
"ἀκούω akoúō, ak-oo´-o; a primary verb; to hear (in various senses):—give (in the) audience (of), come (to the ears), (shall) hear(-er, -ken), be noised, be reported, understand" (Strong 2010, p. 12).

The word translated as *"heard"* is the Greek word *akouo*. As well as the simple act of hearing, as you would hear a sound in the distance and simply recognize that it was a sound, voice, animal, or machine, this word can take on a deeper significance. In addition to hearing is the idea of understanding. The Apostle is saying that those who actually spent time with Jesus came to UNDERSTAND that He was the Christ, in the flesh, God incarnate. That means God in human form. Jesus was 100% God AND 100% human. By hearing Jesus' words, the Apostles came to understand that. And so can we. It took time for them to come to that understanding; they questioned and doubted until they heard His words. The Apostle Paul clearly says the same thing in Romans when he declares that *"faith comes from hearing the message, and the message is heard through the word about Christ"* (Romans 10:17).

See Christ – *"We have seen"*
"ὁράω horáō, hor-ah´-o; properly, to stare at [compare G3700], i.e. (by implication) to discern clearly (physically or mentally); by extension, to attend to; by Hebraism, to experience passively; passively, to appear:—behold, perceive, see, take heed" (Strong 2010, p. 181).

Here again, there is a deeper meaning to the word *"seen"* than just casually noticing something through our sense of vision. Let me hone in on one of the possible applications of this word because I think it hits the heart of what the Apostle is trying to convey. These men and women who spent so much time with Jesus during His life and ministry, they EXPERIENCED Him. This was no chance encounter or simple drive-by meeting on the street. They spent time with Him. They spent years with Him. It was more than just seeing Him at a distance. They experienced the reality of who He really was. I think in today's terms, there are a lot of people who have seen Jesus from a distance. They have been to enough Easter and Christmas services, funerals and weddings, to kind-of see Jesus and know that He is there. However, they have never experienced Him. It would be easy to misunderstand Him if you have never really experienced His presence. That was the mistake of the first-century Gnostics.

Let's not repeat that mistake!

Contemplate Christ – *"We have looked at"*
"θεάομαι theáomai, theh-ah´-om-ahee; a prolonged form of a primary verb; to look closely at, i.e. (by implication) to perceive (literally or figuratively); by extension to visit:—behold, look (upon), see" (Strong 2010, p. 114).

On the surface it would seem that the Apostle has repeated himself. *"We have seen"* and *"we have looked at"* seem to be the same claim, but they are not. These are two different words. He is saying that they have looked closely at who Jesus was and what Jesus claimed. I like the description given by J. Vernon McGee (1983) when he said, "To look, saves; to gaze, sanctifies" (p. 757). This is a profound truth. To gaze on Christ is not a passing glance or even a momentary stare. It is an ongoing practice of looking deeply into who Jesus is and what we need to learn from Him and about Him. A consistent practice of gazing into the word of God through study, and into the heart of God through prayer and contemplation, sanctifies or sets us apart for use by the Holy Spirit. It also sets a Godly perspective into the minds and hearts of any believer!

Handle Christ – *"We have touched"*
"ψηλαφάω psēlapháō, psay-laf-ah´-o; from the base of G5567 (compare G5586); to manipulate, i.e. verify by contact; figuratively, to search for:—feel after, handle, touch" (Strong 2010, p. 275).

Look at these possible applications for the word *"touched."* The disciples of Jesus used their physical experience with Him to base their conviction that He was real; He was a real, physical person who also was Spirit, the living presence of God. They were able to "verify by contact" this core understanding of the person and nature of Christ. They were able to "handle" the word of truth, and they were changed by the experience.

The same can happen for us. We must commit ourselves to the following: (1) hearing the word of Christ in such a way that we can understand, accept, and apply what we hear; (2) seeing Christ by way of a long-term search for who He really is and what that should change within us; (3) contemplating Christ so that we don't miss anything He might have for us; and (4) handling Christ so that we actually physically live out what we have heard, seen, and contemplated. It is then that we will be changed!

Then the world around us will be changed through us.

Day 3

"We proclaim to you what we have seen and heard, so that you also may have fellowship with us. And our fellowship is with the Father and with his Son, Jesus Christ. We write this to make our joy complete." (1 John 1:3-4)

Once again the Apostle John points out that he and the other witnesses like him have *"seen and heard"* the actual, physical, real person of Jesus, who is the Christ. This reality is what John is working to proclaim to everyone who would hear his words or read his letters. This message of Jesus as God incarnate (God in the flesh) is proclaimed to all people so that we can have *"fellowship"* together. This word *"fellowship"* is interesting. The Greek word is *koinonia* and it has the possible translations of partnership, participation, and communion (Blue Letter Bible). These words are much deeper in meaning and context than the way we tend to define them today.

Quite honestly, the word *"fellowship"* is not commonly used today. It was widely used in the church decades ago. I grew up in rather old-school, conservative churches in the southeastern United States. Back then almost every church had a "fellowship hall." This was nothing more than a building with a kitchen and a large meeting room. Most of the time there were tables set up in the large meeting room so that dinners could be served. Quite often we would have potluck dinners. The idea was simple; everyone bring enough for you, your family and one or two more, and we all will have a meal together. We called that *"fellowship."* And so I came to attribute that word with the concept of food and light-hearted, shallow, sometimes awkward, conversation. And I am not alone in this misunderstanding of the word, which has come to mean little more than a church-sponsored party or get-together.

The actual meaning of the word is so much deeper.

Real fellowship cannot be attained with strangers. It is deeper than that. Real fellowship requires shared history, shared experience, shared beliefs, and shared relationships. This cannot be accomplished in a room with a few hundred folks whom you barely know. And it doesn't happen easily in a large group even when you do know everyone.

In 1985, I headed off to college for the first time. I was going to pursue a degree in Music Education. I always had liked music. I had been in choirs and small ensembles all throughout my high school years. I loved to sing. However, when I got to college and began taking classes with other musicians, I discovered something that really shocked me. I found out just how little I actually knew about music! Suddenly, I was surrounded by people who could explain every detail about why a song sounded the way it sounded. They knew how to structure notes, chords, and melodic themes in such a way as to create more than just sounds, but art! I was shocked. I never knew how much I didn't know until I got around people who knew what I didn't know. And that made me better. I began to learn. I began to study, to practice, and to listen. Eventually, I could enter into conversations that most people would never understand. When musicians talk music in ways that non-musicians cannot comprehend, they achieve fellowship.

In 1988, I left that university and moved on to Southern Wesleyan University where I would finish my undergraduate work in Christian Ministries. I entered a school of thought that at first was foreign to me. I had been in church my entire life, but these people were talking about things that I had never heard! Once again, I never knew how much I didn't know until I got around people who knew what I didn't know. And once again, I studied and learned until I had enough shared knowledge and experience that I could enter into fellowship with these people.

Today, I am a pastor. You would think that they taught me all I needed to know about being a pastor in university, but they did not. University taught me how to think. I needed another set of experiences in order to know how to lead. And so I found that group. Once again, I found that I never knew how much I didn't know until I got around people who knew what I didn't know. Now I have fellowship with pastors.

I say all of that to say that fellowship, partnership, participation, and communion all require a shared experience. For the Apostle John, that experience is our personal encounter with the very real, very alive, very human, and very divine person of Jesus who is the Christ! That one singular relationship opens the door to communion with all those who share in the knowledge of His presence, His forgiveness, His power, and His grace! And that communion honestly has nothing to do with food! It has nothing to do with small talk. It has nothing to do with crowds. Now, don't get me wrong; we can find fellowship around a table of food, and often we do. However, the food is not the center of the fellowship; Jesus is! We can have small talk with fellow believers, but the small talk is not what defines the fellowship; Jesus is! We can be deeply moved and changed in large crowds and encounter Jesus and the Holy Spirit in powerful ways, but the crowds are not what defines the experience; Jesus is!

Non-believers gather around food. They do not have the fellowship of knowing Christ.

Non-believers gather in small groups for small talk. They do not have the fellowship of knowing Christ.

Non-believers have powerful experiences in large crowds. They do not have the fellowship of knowing Christ.

The Apostle desires for himself and for all of us: the fellowship of knowing Christ; the partnership among fellow believers; the participation in His body, the church; and the communion of knowing the shared experience of the grace of Jesus and the power of the Holy Spirit. The Gnostic may have an idea about Jesus, but the Apostle KNOWS Him. The world may have a philosophy about Jesus, but the disciple KNOWS Him. Others may have an opinion about Jesus, but we KNOW Him.

And knowing Him makes our joy complete!

Day 4

"This is the message we have heard from him and declare to you: God is light; in him there is no darkness at all." (1 John 1:5)

"God is light." Hear the words properly. God IS light. This is not a statement of what God does. It is a statement of what and who God IS ... He is light. In fact, He is THE light! And light is an absolutely necessary part of our daily existence. Light gives definition and understanding to the world around us. Without light, there can be no real comprehension or understanding. Light takes what is shrouded and shadowy and makes it clear and comprehensible. That is what God does in our lives!

My office is in the back stage area of one of our sanctuary spaces. Unfortunately, there is no light switch next to the door nearest my office. It is always dark in the room when I enter the sanctuary space. I am left with a choice. I can take the door closest to my office and walk through the dark, or I can go farther down the hallway to another sanctuary entrance and turn on the light. Now, I know that room. I know where things are and I know where to walk in order to safely reach my office door. So as long as no one has moved anything, I can easily and safely walk through the dark to my office. However, here's the problem. Often someone will move a chair or leave a prop or a piece of equipment in the walkway. When that happens, I end up stubbing a toe or bruising my shin or falling over what was left in the darkness. If I would take the extra effort to go to the other door and turn on the light, then I would be able to clearly comprehend what was in the walkway and avoid the pain and injury that comes from tripping over things in the dark.

But sometimes that just seems like too much work.

And therein lies the problem.

Today, in our culture, it has become fashionable to argue that there is no God. They would argue that we already know everything we can know about how the world works. We know the walkways and pathways and have studied the world around us so much that we have no need for any God or any light that He might provide. To be honest, on one level, they are right. God, in His graciousness to us, has given us a basic understanding of how the world around us generally works. We simply can use the mind He gave us to study and memorize where the paths are and how to safely journey in this life. Without Him, in the darkness of a life with no God to direct and guide, we tend to run into junk that others have left in our paths. Without warning, our safe path is cluttered with things we cannot see and don't understand. Things that leave us in pain, bruised, bleeding, and confused. Then suddenly, we need light.

God is that light. He provides for us illuminating presence of His Holy Spirit so that we can make sense of the junk that is left in our path. His light and guidance allow us to avoid the obstacles left in our way.

There is more here. The Apostle tells us that *"God is light,"* but then he continues on by saying that *"in him there is no darkness at all."* That is truly good news! Although some might ask: What if God is wrong … or, worse yet, what if God is just messing with us? That is exactly what the Apostle is telling us that we don't have to worry about. God is light and no darkness is in Him. He doesn't mislead or mistreat. He doesn't send us on some pathway just for His own entertainment. He doesn't cause us to do certain things or think certain ways just for His own gain. He cares for us, loves us, and desires what is best for us. He lights our path, and the light and understanding He gives us can be completely trusted!

Day 5

"If we claim to have fellowship with him and yet walk in the darkness, we lie and do not live out the truth. But if we walk in the light, as he is in the light, we have fellowship with one another, and the blood of Jesus, his Son, purifies us from all sin." (1 John 1:6-7)

Since God is light, we should walk in that light.

Walking in that light is liberating!

Simply put, the Christian should always be one who is walking in the light. In fact, if we are walking in darkness while claiming to be in the light (enlightened), then we are living a lie. Now the culture we live in does not accept this understanding of things. In fact, the culture we live in would argue that there is no real difference in walking in darkness and walking in light. To them, one isn't better and another worse; they are just different and neither has greater value. Pressed on the matter, most in our culture would actually argue that walking outside of the word of God or the Bible is better. Even though they can't explain the hurt, brokenness, and emptiness they feel and see in the culture around them.

Think of it this way. God is light, so we should walk in that light in order to keep us from hurting ourselves on things that have been placed in our path unexpectedly. And in God, there is no darkness so we should trust the light He gives us to be good for us. God's ways are not arbitrary or meaningless. They are more than just another way to live. God's ways are right and when God gives us a direction or command, there is always a reason for it.

Think about it for a moment.

Why does God say that we should not lie? (Colossians 3:9). It's because when we lie we cause darkness and death, and when we tell the truth we bring light and life!

Why does God say that we should honor our marriage commitments? (Hebrews 13:4). It's because when we break those commitments we cause darkness, destruction, and death. When we remain true to them we bring light, love, and life!

Why does God say that we should not be drunk on wine? (Ephesians 5:18). It's because drunkenness causes darkness, destruction, and death. When we live sober lives of self-control we bring light, love, and life!

Our culture rejects these very teachings. Our culture actually rewards lying and has decided that it is a necessary part of everyday life. In fact, if you are a better liar than the other guy, our culture thinks you should be given a raise, stardom, or elected to public office. Lying is not an outrage any longer; it is the expected norm! Marriage is no longer viewed as something meant to be cherished for a lifetime. The marriage vows are seen today as little more than temporary promises to be kept as long as it feels good to keep them. When it no longer seems good or fun to keep those vows, they are rejected and traded off for something that feels better, for the moment. Drunkenness has actually become synonymous with fun and partying. Any time there is a party, it is expected that there will be drunkenness. So our society celebrates liars, cheats, and drunks. Then we don't understand why so many people are hurting, lost, confused, broken, addicted, and depressed.

It is because we are living a lie!

Walking in darkness causes pain, destruction, and death.

Walking in light is liberating!

Again, hear the words of the Apostle: *"But if we walk in the light, as he is in the light, we have fellowship with one another, and the blood of Jesus, his Son, purifies us from all sin."* Walking in light brings hope and healing because we find fellowship with other believers who also are striving to walk in the healing light of Jesus Christ. That fellowship gives us the encouragement and strength we desperately need when we suddenly, for whatever reason, find ourselves slipping back into darkness. We stand together, we help each other, we hold each other up, and we hold each other accountable. Why? It is because we are walking together in the light.

Furthermore, there is a promise here. If we are walking in the light, it means we are walking with other believers who will help us. It also means that we are walking with Christ. As we walk with Him, we naturally become more like Him. It's just natural. Whenever you spend great amounts of time with anyone, you begin to think like them, walk like them, talk like them, and act like them. The same is true with Christ. The more we walk in His light, path, and presence, the more we will learn to walk, talk, and act like Him. And that is liberating!

Look, simply put, sin is perfectly designed to bring pain, destruction, and death into your life. The best way to stay far from the darkness of that sin is to walk close to the light of Christ!

So if God is light (and He is!!), then we should walk in that light. Walking in that light is liberating!

Day 6

"If we claim to be without sin, we deceive ourselves and the truth is not in us." (1 John 1:8)

You may be wondering who could possibly claim they are without sin? Well the answer is really two different and yet oddly similar groups. The first group is the collection of people for whom sin just doesn't exist. Our culture is filled with people who refuse to accept the idea that there is a God at all, and therefore they refuse to admit that there is sin at all. For them, anything goes. Although that may seem to be a valid way to view the world, the end result is entirely frightening! If there is no God and therefore no sin, then, by definition, there is no real way to find or understand right and wrong. In fact, right and wrong cannot exist if there is no sin. If there is no wrong, then whatever is best for me is always what is right.

This may sound OK to you until you consider everyone in the world acting on that philosophy. If right is defined as whatever is best for me, then, quite honestly, I have no reason to care for what is best for you. Humanity quickly becomes little more than a smarter group of animals. We hunt, we take, we steal, we hurt, we kill, we defend our territory, and we just don't care what that means or what pain that causes to anyone or anything else. You might say: "Come on pastor! That could never happen! That's just wrong!" Really ... by whose standard? If there is no standard for right, then there can be no standard for wrong.

If there is no definable good, then there can be no definable evil. If there is no God (the standard for good), then there can be no Devil (the standard for evil). If evil cannot be clearly defined, then it cannot be avoided, controlled, fought against, or defeated. So those who argue that there is no God and no sin are walking a dangerous path. Humanity devoid of morality is brilliantly deadly!

The other group that makes this claim is actually Christians. I am a holiness preacher. I come from many generations of holiness preachers. Our church is a holiness church. Now this term likely means little to you since it is not in general use these days. So let me give you a little theological background and then teach a simple lesson. Holiness theology is the belief that after salvation there is another crisis experience that a follower of Christ must go through. This other experience is called by many different names. Wesleyans (our church is Wesleyan) tend to use the term: second definite work of grace. This is different than salvation. At salvation, I am receiving Christ into my life and allowing Him to forgive me of all my sins. At this second definite work of grace, I am not seeking salvation; I am seeking sanctification. Now, that is a big word that means being set apart for sacred use. So when I come to this second decision, I am choosing to set myself apart for God's sacred use. A couple of simple terms might help.

When I get saved (salvation), I get God ... but when I get sanctified, God gets me.

When I get saved (salvation), I give God my sin ... but when I get sanctified, I give God myself.

When this second choice is made and I give myself over to God, I receive from Him the power to live a holy life. *"But if we walk in the light, as he is in the light, we have fellowship with one another, and the blood of Jesus, his Son, purifies* [sanctifies] *us from all sin"* (1 John 1:7). The question is: What changed to allow us to live a holy life? On this question, there are two main schools of thought that I will give you in simple terms to which I have found helpful.

The Victory over Sin Group

This group (I am not in this group) believes that when you come to that second definite work of grace and ask God to sanctify you, God removes the tendency toward sin from which you were born (sin nature). Once that sin nature has been removed, you are free from the tendency that has been a part of your life from birth. Sin is defined as a willful transgression of a known law (sin is something you do on purpose and not by accident). Once the sin nature is removed, you are able to live a life free of sin. So these folks can claim to be without sin. And they do.

The Surrendered to the Spirit Group

This group (I am a part of this group) believes that when you come to that second definite work of grace and ask God to sanctify you, the Holy Spirit is given, by virtue of your choice, full authority in your life. That sin nature is still there, and honestly it always will be on this side of eternity, but it is defeated by your surrender to the Spirit's power. Now, when that temptation comes, and it will, you have chosen and are practicing the art of surrender to the guidance, leadership, nudging, and rebuking of the Holy Spirit. The sin that once defeated you is now defeated, but not by you. It is defeated by the power of the Holy Spirit in you! You have victory only because you surrendered to the One who had victory all along: God!

The difference here is stark. What you believe about yourself has a powerful effect on how you act toward others. The first group (The Victory over Sin Group) believes that they have been completely cured of the sin nature. Because they don't sin, they have really become something special. I mean really! They are awesome, sinless, pure, holy, and godly! The tendency among this group is toward arrogance. In their arrogance, they begin to shun people who are not as holy, and, whether intentional or not, they look down on others. I really can't tell you how many churches and small groups I have seen that ended up like this. The message they give to the world around them is incredibly damaging to the Church in general. Whether they mean to or not (and some really do mean to), they give others the impression that God hates everyone but their little group. I imagine them saying: "All ya'll are just nasty, dirty, vile, little sinners that God can't stand! And until you learn to act, talk, and dress like us, you aren't good enough!" It's just horrible.

Honestly, I would rather hang out with complete sinners than arrogant saints. Instead, I believe that holiness is not a theology of victory; it is a theology of surrender. The saint and the sinner are really not that different. Both have surrendered to something. The sinner has surrendered to the same sins to which the saint used to surrender. Without the power of the Holy Spirit, there is plenty left within the saint to take him or her right back into the sin that once ruled the day. It is our surrender to the Holy Spirit that sets us free. There just isn't any room for arrogance. There's only room for thankfulness. With that comes a very real desire to help everyone who is still caught in the sin that once dominated our lives. They, too, can find the power of the Holy Spirit and surrender to the One who can and will give victory!

God is light and through the power of the Holy Spirit, I can walk in that light and find freedom!

Day 7

"If we confess our sins, he is faithful and just and will forgive us our sins and purify us from all unrighteousness. If we claim we have not sinned, we make him out to be a liar and his word is not in us." (1 John 1:9-10)

Confession.

What does that word mean to you? To many, confession brings up images of going to a church and sitting down across from a priest or pastor and spilling the beans about everything you have done wrong. To others, confession brings up images of some small group or even larger gathering where people confess openly about all of their dirty laundry until there is nothing left to tell. Either way, these images of confession can be, at the very least, awkward and, at the very worst, terrifying!

Confession really isn't about either one of these scenarios. Confession, as it is spoken of here, is not between two people or between you and a group of people. No priest or pastor is required and no small group need be present. Confession is between you and God. In fact, confession is you choosing to agree with God about your sinfulness. I like the way J. Vernon McGee (1983) said this: "When God in His Word says that the thing you did is sin, you are to get over on God's side and look at it. And you are to say, 'You are right, Lord, I say the same thing that You say. It is sin.' That is what it means to confess your sins" (p. 764).

You see, you cannot confess to having done something wrong that you feel wasn't wrong in the first place. At the same time, you cannot get past the sinfulness of sin. Therefore, if we claim that sin is not sinful *("If we claim we have not sinned")*, we are, by definition, calling God a liar: *"We make him out to be a liar and his word is not in us."* It's really quite simple. We either believe God's word or we don't. If we believe God's word, then we must accept that anything He calls sin is actually sinful and requires confession.

Let me dig a little deeper here. Some Christians want to redefine sin. They are constantly looking for loopholes in scripture that might let them do some things that their sinful nature wants to do, even though they know God's word says they shouldn't. This is dangerous ground. To reject God's word is literally to call God a liar. God wrote it. God sent it to us. God preserved it. God made you sit down and read those very words and is banging on the door of your heart right at this moment!! And you feel it.

So what are you going to do about it?

This verse has some amazing good news in it. Look at what John says again in verse nine: *"If we confess our sins, he is faithful and just and will forgive us our sins and purify us from all unrighteousness."* That is really good news! First, bring yourself to agree with God that your sin is actually sinful. Then confess to Him that you need to be forgiven for that sin. As a result, you have a promise from God that He will forgive you

AND purify you from all unrighteousness! That is the best deal you are ever going to be offered. God wants to forgive you. He desires to purify you. He longs to set you free. You need to agree with Him that you need forgiveness, purification, and freedom.

How do you do that?

You simply ask.

I am going to give you a simple prayer that you can use to talk with God, agree with Him about your sinfulness, and ask Him for His forgiveness and purification. Remember, there is nothing magical about these words. The issue is the attitude of your heart, not the arrangement of your words. God always responds to a heart that is sincerely seeking forgiveness. God always purifies a heart that is fully surrendered to Him. God desires to do this for you. Choose to agree with Him about your sinfulness and choose to surrender to Him for your forgiveness.

When you are ready, just pray your **ABCs**:

Admit

"If we confess our sins ..."

Confess to God. Agree with Him about the sinfulness of your actions. Tell Him you are sorry and ask for His forgiveness.

Believe

"He is faithful and just and will forgive us our sins."

Believe that Jesus is willing and able to forgive your sins. Ask Him to wash your life clean and give you a new start.

Commit

"And purify us from all unrighteousness."

Surrender to the Holy Spirit, His word, and His ways in your life so that you can begin becoming more and more like Him. Commit your life to following Him from this day forward no matter what that may mean!

Now you have found the God who is light.

Walk in that light.

Be liberated by that light.

Find that life in Christ is life that is really worth living!

WEEK

2

Day 1

"My dear children, I write this to you so that you will not sin. But if anybody does sin, we have an advocate with the Father— Jesus Christ, the Righteous One. He is the atoning sacrifice for our sins, and not only for ours but also for the sins of the whole world." (1 John 2:1-2)

What an amazing phrase: *"I write this to you so that you will not sin."* There is an assumption made here that we need to unpack. Last week, I talked about the definition of sin. Today, let's dig a little deeper into that issue. Sin is a concept that arises in almost every religious theology. In Christianity, the concept of sin is, at its core, simple to understand. Sin is a violation of God's law. However, that simple understanding turns out to be a little more complex. There really are two main thoughts when it comes to the definition of sin. Let me very simply explain them and then show you how they apply to the verse we are dealing with here.

Definition #1: Sin is any falling short of the glory of God.

This is a really high standard. In fact, it is an impossible standard. In this definition of sin, sin can simply not be avoided. It happens every minute of every day. Every time I do something that is less than the perfect standard of God, I sin. If I misspell a word and have to go back and correct it ... that would be falling short of God's perfect glory, so I suppose that would be sin. Now while that particular example may be a little overboard, you get the picture. Each of us falls short of God's perfect glory every day. In fact, those who hold to this definition of sin have a saying: "We sin every day in word, thought, and deed." For them, sin is just part of the human existence. However, this daily pattern of sin in "word, thought, and deed" is not fatal to the Christian life or salvation. The blood of Christ is sufficient to cover this constant flow of sin. So ultimately, the end result is the same regardless of the definition of sin. The blood of Jesus sacrificed for us on the cross pays the price of our sins and we need only to accept His forgiveness.

There is a bit of a challenge here. Our verse today says: *"My dear children, I write this to you so that you will not sin."* If we can't help but sin, what does this verse mean? How could we ever live out this verse if we automatically sin every day in word, thought, and deed? How could we ever *"not sin"* (John's words, not mine) if sin is any falling short of the glory of God? I find these questions too difficult to answer. For that reason, and many others that we won't get into here, I don't adhere to this definition of sin.

Definition #2: Sin is a willful transgression of a known law.

Let's work with this standard. If sin is a willful transgression (an offense) of a known law, then sin is something done on purpose, not by accident. In this definition, sin becomes a simple act of rebellion. I know what God said I should do. I know what I am supposed to do. I am choosing to do otherwise. That is sin. It is chosen and then acted upon. That moment of choosing may be no more than a split second, but the choice is made nonetheless. Now, if sin is something done on purpose, then it is not necessarily true that a person must "sin every day in word, thought, and deed." In fact, it is conceivable that a person could possibly go through a 24-hour period without willfully transgressing a known law of God. In this definition of sin, our verse here in 1 John makes more sense: *"My dear children, I write this to you so that you will not sin."* Now using this definition, what John writes to us is actually possible!

In fact, I believe that this second definition is the one that is most helpful in understanding much of scripture. Understanding sin as rebellion against God squares up so many stories. From Lucifer who rebelled against God to become Satan, to Adam and Eve in the Garden of Eden, to Samson in Judges, to King David in 1 and 2 Samuel, to the Nation of Israel in the Old Testament, to Ananias and Sapphira in the book of Acts, we see the consistent truth that sin is willful rebellion against God. I actually would challenge you to find a sin in scripture that was not the result of a willful transgression of a known law. Sin is rebellion. The Apostle John is writing to us specifically so that we will not rebel! He is begging us not to sin. He is imploring us to *"walk in the light, as he is in the light"* and to allow God to *"purify us from all unrighteousness"* (1 John 1:7, 9).

I find a real hope and solid goal in this understanding of sin. If it is possible that I might be able to make it through the next 24 hours without rebellion against God (without sin), then that is what I am going to strive to do. When that 24 hours is done, I'm going to try again! I know that I can't keep it up forever. I just ain't that good! And neither are you. So the Apostle goes on in the next verse: *"But if anybody does sin, we have an advocate with the Father—Jesus Christ, the Righteous One."* Wow! For God's glory, I can strive to go without sin (willful rebellion) for as long as I possibly can. That will bring glory to God and make my life infinitely better. AND when I do mess up, Jesus is going to forgive me and act as my defense attorney to His Father, God.

That is really good news! And it is for everyone when he says, *"and not only for ours* [our sin] *but also for the sins of the whole world."* The Apostle makes it clear that God's forgiveness, God's grace, God's power to live free from the bondage of sin, and God's purifying presence is available to everyone in the entire world!

That means you.

Hey, how about we start our first 24 hours now?

Day 2

"We know that we have come to know him if we keep his commands. Whoever says, 'I know him,' but does not do what he commands is a liar, and the truth is not in that person. But if anyone obeys his word, love for God is truly made complete in them. This is how we know we are in him: Whoever claims to live in him must live as Jesus did. Dear friends, I am not writing you a new command but an old one, which you have had since the beginning. This old command is the message you have heard. Yet I am writing you a new command; its truth is seen in him and in you, because the darkness is passing and the true light is already shining." (1 John 2:3-8)

There are those who say that they know God, believe in God, and love God, but they are not living in biblical truth. Let me be clear, when I say living in biblical truth, I am not talking about some legalistic expectation of living in perfection. I mean that there are a lot of people who are living in blatant, obvious rebellion against God's word while still claiming they are Christians.

These two things cannot co-exist.

The Apostle John is clearly reminding us of something that He learned directly from Jesus. Jesus' words recorded in John's Gospel lay out the original command: *"If you love me, keep my commands"* (John 14:15). Love for God plays out in how we live our lives. Our love for God should affect every part of how we live our lives. It just isn't a rational point of view to say that we love Him and yet consistently violate what He desires for us. If you love Him, you will follow Him and obey Him. I know we don't like the sound of the word "obey." Nevertheless, it is a part of how we show love to those who have charge over us. When we were young, we obeyed our parents, or at least we should have. Our obedience was part of our love for them. We loved them and did not want to hurt them, so we obeyed them. This same type of relationship plays out with God.

The choice to obey Him has a natural outcome. We will become more like Him. Read these words again: *"But if anyone obeys his word, love for God is truly made complete in them."* When we obey Him, the work of our maturity is being made complete. We are being made more and more like Him. Until finally these words are lived out through us: *"This is how we know we are in him: Whoever claims to live in him must live as Jesus did."* Again, this is like our relationship with our parents. We obeyed them because we loved them. The more we obeyed them and loved them, the more we became like them. Until the day comes when we, as adults, hear our own voices and in complete shock realize that we sound just like our parents! We think: Oh no! It's happening! I'm becoming my Mom!! And it's true. We become like them because we learn from them and we love them.

And so it should be with God.

People sometimes ask me if I can give them some type of spiritual growth guide, schedule, or plan. I know a lot of pastors who have guides or plans, but I don't. I think if you want to grow to be more like Christ, you should just spend more time with Him through prayer, reading His word, worshipping Him, and hanging out with His children. I think the more you hang with Jesus, the more you will be like Jesus. That is exactly how it worked in John's life. He and the other disciples spent three years living with, hanging out with, working with, and struggling with Jesus. Over that time, they became more like Him. John points out that this concept is nothing new. This idea of obeying God because we love God is not a new command. It has been around since Moses and was clearly the expectation of Jesus.

"Yet I am writing you a new command; its truth is seen in him and in you, because the darkness is passing and the true light is already shining."

This old command is now new because we are on the other side of the cross. Jesus died for our sins and redemption and forgiveness is ours for the asking. More importantly, Jesus has risen from the grave and defeated the death and sin that once dominated our existence. He has renewed our relationship with God and has set a clear pathway for us to reconnect with our Creator. Perhaps most importantly for our daily walks, He has sent the Holy Spirit to come alongside us every moment of every day. God, our Creator, sent Jesus, our Savior, who in turn sent the Holy Spirit, our Helper.

So there is no excuse. God has created you for a grand purpose. Jesus has forgiven you for everything you have ever done wrong, and He gives you a new chance at life. The Holy Spirit will help you see the world from God's perspective and navigate through what was once complete darkness. Now *"the darkness is passing and the true light* [God is light] *is already shining."* All of this, God has done and is doing for you. Show Him you love Him by obeying His commands.

Day 3

"Anyone who claims to be in the light but hates a brother or sister is still in the darkness. Anyone who loves their brother and sister lives in the light, and there is nothing in them to make them stumble. But anyone who hates a brother or sister is in the darkness and walks around in the darkness. They do not know where they are going, because the darkness has blinded them." (1 John 2:9-11)

Many years ago, I had a falling out with another pastor who was a friend. I really didn't harbor any resentment toward him, but at the time I was pretty hurt by the circumstances, as I'm sure he was. I sat down with my mom and told her all about it because he was one of the pastors at her church, and my whole family went to that church. I had to make sure they knew that I wasn't going to harbor any ill will toward this man, their pastor. In short, I was really upset over the whole incident. I didn't want to hinder his ministry or my family's ability to be ministered. So I talked to Mom. A few weeks later, my mom and I were talking about the situation again. I asked her what my Grandpa Freeman thought about it. (He went to the church too!) She said: "Oh, Michael!" (Mom always starts sentences that way when she thinks I have said or done something less than wise.) "I didn't tell your Grandpa about it! He would never understand why two men of God couldn't get along!" And that was the end of the conversation. I have to tell you, that moment cut me, warmed me, and taught me. These lessons perfectly align with this section of scripture.

"Anyone who claims to be in the light but hates a brother or sister is still in the darkness."

It cut me because I had the capacity to understand how two ministers could be angry at each other, hold resentment toward each other, and almost hate each other, at least for a time ... but Grandpa didn't. I have always wanted to be like him. He just loved people. It was so natural to him to love everyone. And then to realize that his love for people was so deep and real that he wouldn't even be able to comprehend how to two brothers in Christ could be angry ... just made me long even more to be like him. Then I remembered that according to this verse, if I were to allow that anger and resentment to fester within me and become hatred, then the darkness that God had delivered me from would creep back into my life and steal from me the light that I so loved and valued. I realized that I could not hold my resentment toward that man and still walk in the light of Christ. Let me be more direct. I had to choose. Was I going to walk in the light of God or was I going to walk in the heat of anger? I could not do both. I had to choose. And so do you.

"Anyone who loves their brother and sister lives in the light, and there is nothing in them to make them stumble."

It warmed me because I realized that this kind of godliness really is possible. It really is possible to love people and have that love become so natural, real, and intuitively normal that anything but love is inconceivable. I realized that there is a much, much deeper place that I could strive for, and through the grace of God and presence of the Holy Spirit, one day arrive. I realized that I had a lot of work to do, but there is hope! Then I remembered that there was a promise that went along with this kind of love. When we learn to love like God loves, we walk so clearly in the light that there is NOTHING to make us stumble! Did you hear that? In that kind of love, the light is so clear and bright that you couldn't possibly stumble. Then the things that so often destroy the spiritual lives of so many Christians (hatred, anger, malice, discord, resentment, and not being able to forgive) can't even get traction in your life because you are so overwhelmingly controlled by love. That's awesome!

"But anyone who hates a brother or sister is in the darkness and walks around in the darkness. They do not know where they are going, because the darkness has blinded them."

It taught me that I should NEVER allow my hurt feelings from any situation or individual challenge the love that Christ is working out in my heart. Let me say it again. You have to choose between walking in the light of God or in the heat of anger. You cannot do both at the same time. If you should choose to harbor anger and resentment just because you have the right to, you open the door to the darkness of hatred. When hatred takes control, darkness is already firmly in place. The love of God drives out the darkness. Remember, God is light and in Him there is no darkness at all. When we choose the darkness of hatred, we reject the light of God.

We have to choose. I'm just going tell you that the world would be a much better place if there were more Grandpa Freemans around. I want to be that man who can't imagine how two Christians could possibly harbor anger and resentment toward each other, as if it was just too much to process or too foreign a thought to possibly be entertained. How wonderful would that be?

Dear God,

Make me like Grandpa.

Michael

Day 4

"I am writing to you, dear children, because your sins have been forgiven on account of his name. I am writing to you, fathers, because you know him who is from the beginning. I am writing to you, young men, because you have overcome the evil one. I write to you, dear children, because you know the Father. I write to you, fathers, because you know him who is from the beginning. I write to you, young men, because you are strong, and the word of God lives in you, and you have overcome the evil one." (1 John 2:12-14)

Here the Apostle explains whom he is writing to and why. This time he speaks to different groups of believers. He breaks it down here into three sections and then speaks to each group two times. Honestly, as you read over this you will likely discover that you are clearly in at least one of these groups. Your placement in that group will help determine what your focus should be in your spiritual development. So let's take a look at them one at a time.

Children

"I am writing to you, dear children, because your sins have been forgiven on account of his name" and *"because you know the Father."*

The Apostle John starts with *"dear children."* The Greek word here literally means little child (Blue Letter Bible). He explains what defines this group. Their knowledge of God is rather limited. They know they have been *"forgiven on account of his name"* and they *"know the Father."* These are folks who have found salvation in Christ, but that is about the limit of it. Now, in your mind you have already gone to the children's ministry area of the church; you are hearing the Apostle speak of little children as if he were speaking of someone's age. However, he is not. He is speaking of the levels of spiritual maturity between these three groups, not the number of years lived by these three groups. It is altogether possible that there would be people included in the *"dear children"* category who are adults, middle-aged, or even old folk!

As much as I hate to admit it, I have run into this phenomenon through the years. All too often, regardless of age or the number of years in church, I run into some *"dear children."* On one level, I suppose that's OK. At least they believe, are saved, and heaven bound! On many other levels, it really isn't OK. If our children fail to grow, we seek professional help, as we should. There is a problem if there isn't growth. The same is true for our spiritual lives. A person's faith should be growing, developing, and maturing over time. Something is wrong if growth isn't taking place. One should seek treatment or a professional. Something needs to change! We must be growing. While we all start out as *"dear children,"* we cannot stay there!

Young Men
"I am writing to you, young men, because you have overcome the evil one" and *"because you are strong, and the word of God lives in you."*

The word *"young men"* refers to someone who is at the age of learning, such as an attendant or a steward (Blue Letter Bible). In other words, we are dealing with someone who has grown past *"dear children"* but has not yet reached full maturity. Many, if not most, Christians are in this category. We are striving, learning, experiencing, and chasing. We are strong and have, in many ways, overcome temptation and evil, but we still have a long way to go. Honestly, physical youth is no excuse for spiritual weakness. Young men and women have been at the forefront of many of history's greatest revivals. It makes sense that this is true. Again, the Apostle is not really referring to physical age. No matter what our actual age or level of spiritual development, look at the secret we can find here: *"You are strong, and the word of God lives in you."* Our strength and thereby our ability to *"overcome the evil one"* comes from the word of God that lives in us! It should be noted here that the Apostle Paul taught the same thing in Ephesians. As he describes the armor of God, there is only one offensive weapon given: *"the sword of the Spirit, which is the word of God"* (Ephesians 6:17). Every other thing that the Apostle Paul talks about is a defensive piece of armor, but the word of God is the weapon that we can use to *"overcome the evil one."*

Fathers
"I am writing to you, fathers, because you know him who is from the beginning."

Both of the other groups had something added to their list when the Apostle John wrote to them the second time. The Fathers do not. No change. No addition. Simply that they *"know him who is from the beginning."* Then again, there is nothing more needed. To know Christ is the ultimate goal of all followers of Christ. Listen to the Apostle Paul again, but this time from his letter to the Philippians: *"I want to know Christ—yes, to know the power of his resurrection and participation in his sufferings, becoming like him in his death, and so, somehow, attaining to the resurrection from the dead"* (Philippians 3:10-11). Then there's this verse earlier in Philippians: *"For to me, to live is Christ and to die is gain"* (1:21). Paul had no death wish. He simply understood something that the Apostle John is teaching us here. The goal of the Christian is to know Christ. When we have come to truly know Him, we have become one of the Fathers of the faith to the group God has given us. So how do we come to know Christ?

Time.

There are no Fathers who are young. It takes time to know Christ this way. By this, I mean years, even decades. There is nothing quite like being prayed over by a man or woman who has served their God faithfully for decades. That person just knows how to talk to God. They know how to pray for you. Their time with God and years of following Him have made their experience and knowledge invaluable and irreplaceable. When you find people like that, take my advice and keep them around! They are worth your time. They will make you better. Why? Because they know Him!

Day 5

"Do not love the world or anything in the world. If anyone loves the world, love for the Father is not in them. For everything in the world—the lust of the flesh, the lust of the eyes, and the pride of life—comes not from the Father but from the world. The world and its desires pass away, but whoever does the will of God lives forever." (1 John 2:15-17)

"Do not love the world." The Apostle is not suggesting that we should hate the world or be dismissive of the world. At least not in the way we are hearing the term. We hear the term and we think about people. God wants us to love people. I think we have clearly seen that in this chapter of 1 John, and we will see more of it in the chapters to come. The Apostle is not speaking of creation itself either. God gave us this wonderful and amazing world to live in, and we should love it and take care of it. The Apostle is speaking of the societal structures and philosophical ideas that are in opposition to God and godliness.

I have spoken many times (some in this book) about how our culture is, at the least, uncomfortable with biblical truth and, at times, downright hostile toward biblical truth. Much of current culture sees the Bible, the Church, and our God as a threat to their way of life. They view biblical truth as outdated, bigoted, shallow, and narrow-minded. They view us as ignorant simpletons without enough mental strength of our own to function without the fairytale of God. That system of thought and understanding is what

John tells us we cannot love, and the reason is quite simple. One cannot love the system that demands the destruction of God while loving God at the same time. It just doesn't work that way.

The Apostle then reminds us that all of these ideas and cultural norms are temporary. They are temporary in two different ways. First of all, *"the lust of the flesh, the lust of the eyes, and the pride of life"* are temporary because they are of the physical world and not the spiritual world. We have misunderstood what is really real. We somehow have determined that what we can see, touch, and handle is what is real, which isn't the case. Everything of this physical world is temporary. Physical humans are temporary. Buildings are temporary. Governments and even nations are temporary. They all tend to decay and pass away. The spiritual world is eternal. The soul that lives inside a physical body is what is real because that is what will last forever. The *"lust of the flesh"* is temporary. Honestly, many of those lusts will disappear before the body stops functioning! The *"lusts of the eyes"* is temporary. In fact, this temptation will change constantly as your eyes will lust different things at different times in your life. When I was younger, my eyes lusted after cars that sat low to the ground and drove really fast! When I became a parent, my eyes lusted after a car that had plenty of room, high up off the road, and safe for my kids. Today, I just want a car that has a seat that will warm my rear on a cold morning. These eyes change constantly. And the pride of life is a shifting target as well. There was a time when I wanted to be rich. Then a time I wanted to be famous. Now, I just want to be loved and respected by my children and family. All of this stuff is temporary and changing. Therefore, it is not worthy of our love. Only God is worthy of our love.

Secondly, all of these things are temporary because the way culture thinks is constantly shifting. Once again, let me point out that these godless ways of thinking are not new. Societies throughout history have come to think the way we do today. There is a pattern of becoming "too smart" to believe in God, beginning to follow the norms and morals of some other people group around us, or simply make up our own new morals and norms until we finally see our sinfulness. That sinfulness will begin to decay away the foundations of our society. This decay will ultimately lead to the collapse of our decayed culture, and then we will start the cycle over as we run back to God in our distress. This pattern repeats itself over and over again in the Old Testament. So for us to act like we somehow just figured all this out because of how smart we are is just dumb.

"The world and its desires pass away, but whoever does the will of God lives forever."

And so it is. When we follow God's will. When we develop God's presence in our lives. When we become more like Him, we are investing in that part of us that lives forever. The truth is that there was a time when we **were not** (before we were born), but there will never again be a time when we **are not** (eternal beings). We will live forever somewhere. Today is the day to choose to live forever in the presence of God. That choice will demand that we fall out of love with this world, so that we can fall even deeper in love with the God who already has chosen to love us.

Day 6

"Dear children, this is the last hour; and as you have heard that the antichrist is coming, even now many antichrists have come. This is how we know it is the last hour. They went out from us, but they did not really belong to us. For if they had belonged to us, they would have remained with us; but their going showed that none of them belonged to us." (1 John 2:18-19)

In this section, the Apostle John is really speaking to us about two different groups of people that are connected by deception. The first is *"the antichrist,"* the deceiver. The second are the ones who *"went out from us,"* the deceived. Let's unpack both.

The Deceiver – the antichrist

Don't get lost in this word. In today's pop culture, the word antichrist is understood to exclusively mean the spokesman of Satan who will usher in the end of all time. That is not what the Apostle John is speaking to here. While I know some will disagree with me, I don't think John is intentionally referencing the end of days right here in the middle of his teaching on being followers of Christ. I think when John speaks of the antichrist, he is not speaking of a particular individual. Listen to his description later in the same letter: *"Every spirit that acknowledges that Jesus Christ has come in the flesh is from God, but every spirit that does not acknowledge Jesus is not from God. This is the spirit of the antichrist"* (1 John 4:2-3). So here John is warning his *"dear children"* to watch out for the antichrists who are actively trying to lead them away from a true and right understanding of Jesus. And there were plenty of them in John's day!

Sometimes we think that being a Christian must certainly be more difficult today than it has ever been, but I don't think that is true. I believe that every generation has had to struggle with difficult and confusing things as they pursued God. The first-century Christians are no exception. They are hearing that Jesus is not God, Jesus is a heathen, and Jesus is only kind-of God from people who claim to have some kind of special knowledge that gives them power to know and direct the hand of Jesus!! These first-century Christians are desperately trying to sort it all out, and this is why the Apostle John writes this very letter. This is why he made such a big deal at the outset about having spent time with Jesus, having seen Him, touched Him, and walked with Him. John is pleading with these *"dear children"* of his not to listen to the voices that are against Jesus (antichrist), so that they will not be lead astray.

Today, we face many of the same voices. They still call out to lead us away from Christ. Some demand that we reject the very existence of Christ while others demand that we reject the significance of Christ. Some claim to know Him and claim that we must follow them because they know Him better than us; they act as though they have gained some special knowledge that makes them, their faith, and their power superior to us.

Same stories ... different era ... all antichrists ... not the end of the world.

The Deceived – the ones who went out from us

It is truly possible to be deceived. It is also possible to allow that deception to drag you away from the grace of Christ and the family of God. John clearly describes this tragedy: *"They went out from us, but they did not really belong to us. For if they had belonged to us, they would have remained with us; but their going showed that none of them belonged to us."* Sometimes people are more committed to what they want to believe than what they ought to believe. When that happens, they are constantly looking for someone who is willing to say what they want to hear. The Apostle Paul vividly points this out when he is writing to his student, Timothy. *"For the time will come when people will not put up with sound doctrine. Instead, to suit their own desires, they will gather around them a great number of teachers to say what their itching ears want to hear"* (2 Timothy 4:3). We can easily be deceived by our own desire for a truth and therefore a god made in our own image. Such a truth cannot save us. In fact, that kind of truth is the spirit of the antichrist. That kind of truth, which actually isn't truth at all, will destroy us.

The warning here is really two-fold:

1. Don't be an antichrist. Be careful what you teach people about Jesus. Always check and double check that you are teaching a biblical reality and

not simply a personal preference. There is a cost to leading astray one of the *"dear children."* Jesus himself spelled this out clearly when He said to his disciples: *"Things that cause people to stumble are bound to come, but woe to anyone through whom they come. It would be better for them to be thrown into the sea with a millstone tied around their neck than to cause one of these little ones to stumble. So watch yourselves"* (Luke 17:1-3).

2. Don't allow yourself to be deceived by one of these people. The word of God is available to you. Check and double check what a preacher, including this one, has to say to you about Christ. Don't just take a person at their word. Read it for yourself. Look into it. You will be protected from being deceived and will grow personally in the process.

Day 7

"But you have an anointing from the Holy One, and all of you know the truth. I do not write to you because you do not know the truth, but because you do know it and because no lie comes from the truth. Who is the liar? It is whoever denies that Jesus is the Christ. Such a person is the antichrist—denying the Father and the Son. No one who denies the Son has the Father; whoever acknowledges the Son has the Father also. As for you, see that what you have heard from the beginning remains in you. If it does, you also will remain in the Son and in the Father. And this is what he promised us—eternal life. I am writing these things to you about those who are trying to lead you astray. As for you, the anointing you received from him remains in you, and you do not need anyone to teach you. But as his anointing teaches you about all things and as that anointing is real, not counterfeit—just as it has taught you, remain in him. And now, dear children, continue in him, so that when he appears we may be confident and unashamed before him at his coming. If you know that he is righteous, you know that everyone who does what is right has been born of him." (1 John 2:20-29)

As we look at this rather long reading today, I believe we can find a pattern to be followed. In this pattern, we will be able to defend our faith and stay the course for this long-haul marathon called the Christian life. And you need to remember that. The Christian life is more than just a service, a seminar, or an emotional moment at the end of a sermon or retreat. The Christian life is a day-to-day, long pursuit of knowing Christ better today than I did yesterday. If we are going to make it through that, we better have a plan, and the Apostle John gives us an outline for such a plan.

You Have an Anointing

"But you have an anointing from the Holy One."

This word *"anointing"* is the Greek word *chrisma* (Blue Letter Bible). The idea behind this word is something smeared on like an ointment or salve. This concept would be completely familiar to his first-century audience. They have seen anointing ceremonies where oil or salve was smeared onto a leader or elder to indicate the covering and empowering presence of the Lord. It is saying to them that they have the presence and power of the Holy Spirit smeared over them. He is with them, soaking into them, protecting them, and guiding them. Like any other oily ointment, He does not easily wash off. This Holy Spirit anointing is the lasting protection that these Christians know they need. And so it is for us. When we receive Christ at salvation and then surrender our lives to Him in sanctification, He smears the presence of the Holy Spirit over, around, and through our lives. The Holy Spirit is always with us, in us, protecting us, and guiding us. He is here to stay!

Remember this when the days get tough, and surrender to Him when the temptation gets difficult.

You Know the Truth

"I do not write to you because you do not know the truth, but because you do know it."

To these first-century Christians, the Apostle assures them that since they have his letter and the letters from the other Apostles, they have the truth (the real truth). It is the truth that came from those who received it directly from the presence of Jesus, our Savior. Since they know the truth, they can discern between the truth of God and the lies of antichrists. In the same way, we have the truth. Today, antichrists come in the form of people who want to distort or dismiss the truth of scripture. These people try to convince us that they are just so smart that we should listen to them and let go of our old-fashioned, simplistic ideas about God. Let me assure you of something. The truth of God's word has been around for 2,000 plus years since Jesus, and it was around in the form of the Old Testament for as many as 1,500 years before that. There has never, in all those years, been a shortage of people who were so smart that they wanted to dismiss God's word. Today, you don't know their names, but you do know the truth. So I ask you: Which seems smarter to you? Ideas that come and go or the word of God that always remains unchanged, unmoved, and never undone?

You have the truth ... remember it ... and put it in practice.

Hold your Ground
"As for you, see that what you have heard from the beginning remains in you."

The Apostle reminds them of something that we would do well to remember. There will be days when remaining in our faith will simply require the stubborn act of remaining. The anointing is on you, so the Holy Spirit can guide and teach you everything you need to know. Through scripture, prayer, sermons, studies, songs and inspiration, the Holy Spirit will speak to you and teach you. Listen for Him everywhere. When you think you have heard from the Holy Spirit, compare that to scripture to be sure you are hearing properly. But know this, your faith and your truth comes from the Holy Spirit of God. Stubbornly hold on to Him and His truth. Make Him yours, and make His truth yours. Stubbornly refuse to give in to the antichrists who will always be flitting around with another "brilliant" idea.

Continue in Him

"And now, dear children, continue in him, so that when he appears we may be confident and unashamed before him at his coming. If you know that he is righteous, you know that everyone who does what is right has been born of him."

Our faith is more than just an internal, mental, or spiritual exercise. Our faith is a practical, physical out-play of the mental and spiritual experience with the truth of God, His spirit, and His word.

If your faith **does not** work, then your faith **will not** work.

In other words, those who do not act on their faith tend to lose their faith. Eventually, a completely internalized faith loses its grip on the reality of day-to-day life. It becomes something that you put in a box and pull out whenever you need it. Over time, you seem to need it less and less.

When Tina and I were first married in 1988, one of our first purchases together was a Christmas nativity set. We decided that we would purchase this while we were on our honeymoon, which was in Mexico. So as we shopped around for a nativity set, everything we found looked strikingly Mayan. I suppose this shouldn't have surprised me, but I was young and every nativity I had ever seen had the folks looking strikingly European. After I thought about it, that wasn't right either! So we bought one. We still have that nativity set. In the first few years, we put it out every year. People thought it was a little odd and funny, so we would tell them the story of where we got it. It was our little nativity. Tiny. Mexican. Poorly painted. Cheap.

And we brought it out once a year.

In fact, since then, we have bought and been given many nativities. Most are nicer than the one we bought in 1988, so our little Mayan nativity set never comes out anymore. We just have it.

And so it is with too many people's faith. They have it. It is stored away in some special place waiting to be brought out on some special day when they can tell some special story to some special group of people who are gathered at the house for some special reason. But that isn't how faith is supposed to work. Faith isn't meant just for special occasions. It's meant for every occasion.

That same year, Tina and I bought cookware. I worked as a salesman for a cookware company, so we got a really big discount and bought an entire set. I didn't buy it as some keepsake or statement, the way I bought the little nativity; I bought it to use. Every day, I pulled out some piece of that cookware and used it. Today, I still use that same cookware. The handles are faded and many of them are cracked or slightly broken, but it is still good cookware and in constant use. They're usually full of food and sometimes dirty piled in the sink, but they're used. Somehow, I think that is how our faith should look. Not pristine and protected in some box waiting for some special day, but dirty, used, and full of nourishment.

Remember, if your faith does not work, then your faith will not work.

So put your faith to work and be amazed at how long and effective your faith works!

WEEK

3

Day 1

"See what great love the Father has lavished on us, that we should be called children of God! And that is what we are! The reason the world does not know us is that it did not know him." (1 John 3:1)

There is a story in the Gospels of Matthew, Mark, Luke, and John. It is repeated by each of them and gives us an image of what the Apostle is talking about here. The story is of a woman named Mary who enters the room as Jesus is reclining at the table with His disciples. In John's Gospel, he recalls the moment like this: *"Then Mary took about a pint of pure nard, an expensive perfume; she poured it on Jesus' feet and wiped his feet with her hair. And the house was filled with the fragrance of the perfume"* (John 12:3).

I would like to use this story as a framework to understand today's verse.

Extravagant Love
"See what great love the Father has lavished on us."

When Mary walked into the room that day with this *"pint of pure nard,"* she walked in with her life's treasure in her hands. This was the best thing she had. According to the other Gospel accounts, it was worth a year's wages. In 2014 U.S. dollar values, that would be a pint of perfume valued at $53,657. In the Gospel of John, he said *"she poured it on Jesus' feet."* She didn't carefully place a drop or two. She didn't delicately dab a small smear on the top of his foot; no, she poured it all out on his feet. A $53,000 gesture of love and devotion lavishly and freely spilled out onto the Savior's feet.

I think this moment is in John's mind as he pens the words: *"See what great love the Father has lavished on us."* God did not just place a Band-Aid on our needs. He did not send a lowly angel to help us manage our sin. He did not just look lovingly on as we struggled wishing He could do something. He lavished the life of His one and only son, Jesus. While Mary's gift was extravagant, it pales in comparison to the gift of Christ. Jesus is the *"great love the Father has lavished on us."* He took the most precious and valuable thing and gave it to us. Jesus took His life and he poured it out for us. His blood was poured out for our forgiveness. And when all of that was done, when Jesus was raised and death and hell defeated, God poured out His Holy Spirit on us! Not just a dab. Not just a drop or two, but a downpour of the precious and powerful presence of God. A rainstorm of God's favor so thick and strong that no one can escape the sense that something has changed.

Oh ... what great love ... lavished on us!

Incredible Honor
"That we should be called children of God! And that is what we are!"

Notice two things about Mary's offering. First of all, *"she poured it on Jesus' feet."* She was washing His feet with $53,000 worth of perfume! Foot washing was a very common thing in her day. It was a ritual generally performed by the lowest servant available and was considered a rather insulting job. So the act of foot washing included the lowest of servants serving the most important of guests pouring out the least valuable of liquids.

Do you see it?

Mary took a mundane, even lowly, act and turned it into an extreme and extravagant show of devotion and honor. Imagine the thought in her mind: If the feet of important men are to be washed with water, then the feet of this man shall be washed with liquid gold! Then, instead of a towel to dry His feet, she reached down with her own hair and wiped the now beautifully fragrant mud, dirt, and filth from the feet of her Savior. This act in the first century is more profound than you currently understand. In that culture, a woman's hair was her honor or her glory (1 Corinthians 11:15). Therefore, she has just taken all of her wealth and all of her honor and spent it in a moment to clean the feet of Jesus. The fragrance that identifies him now identifies her. She is inextricably bound to the presence of this man. She is identified with Him. That connection, identity, relationship, and sacrifice will soon cost Jesus His life; it now costs Mary her honor.

Our honor, our identity, our very name is inextricably bound with the name of Jesus. We are sons and daughters of God. He called us that, and since He said it, it is true. Our honor is of no value. Our worth is of no value. Until, somehow, it is poured out onto Him. Then the dirt and muddy grime of our wayward journey fills any room we enter with the stunning, beautiful fragrance of the presence of Christ.

Unbelievable Truth

"The reason the world does not know us is that it did not know him."

The disciples who were there at the moment didn't get it, at least some of them didn't. The Bible said they complained: *"Why this waste?... This perfume could have been sold at a high price and the money given to the poor"* (Matthew 26:8-9). Jesus understood, and then He explained: *When she poured this perfume on my body, she did it to prepare me for burial. Truly I tell you, wherever this gospel is preached throughout the world, what she has done will also be told, in memory of her"* (Matthew 26:12-13).

Honestly, the world doesn't get it. They cannot understand why we would devote our lives to follow this man, Jesus. They don't understand why we would give, and sometimes give extravagantly, to this body of Christ known as the Church. They don't understand nor can begin to imagine why we would sacrifice to serve in the name of Christ.

They don't understand us, because they don't know Him.

They sense something different, something beautiful, something ... well ... something.

In the timeline of this event with Mary, she anoints Jesus with perfume just before Jesus is arrested and crucified. Can you imagine? The fragrance of Mary's sacrifice journeyed with the Savior all the way to the cross. The temple guards who arrested him must have wondered: What is that beautiful smell? The Sanhedrin and High Priest who were condemning Him must have noticed the beautiful fragrance that was for some reason wafting through the room. The soldiers who were beating him must have wondered: Where is that smell coming from? Even the soldiers standing at the foot of the cross would have caught a whiff of something beautiful intermingled with the sweat, blood, and dirt of the moment. They didn't really understand. They didn't get it. They caught just enough to realize that even in the midst of this anger, hatred and horror, something beautiful lingered.

And that is who we are. We are the *"children of God"* and it is the extravagant gift of Jesus that has been *"lavished on us."* Although the world doesn't really get it, we are the sweet, beautiful aroma of the presence of the God who is our Savior, our Honor, our Hope, and worthy of our absolute best. We linger in the air of any culture we indwell. The aroma of our Savior's love and our God's provision wafts through the halls of our business and the back alleyways of our daily journey. We are the very fragrance of God intermingled with the sweat, blood, anger, hatred, and horror of a world that desperately seeks something beautiful.

We are the children of God.

Day 2

"Dear friends, now we are children of God, and what we will be has not yet been made known. But we know that when Christ appears, we shall be like him, for we shall see him as he is. All who have this hope in him purify themselves, just as he is pure." (1 John 3:2-3)

"Dear friends, now we are children of God."

What a great statement! The Apostle makes it clear that *"now we are children of God."* Now. We are currently listed as the children of the King of Kings! That should affect the way we act. Quite simply, we often fail to act like we are who God says we are. Let me remind you of something I say quite often. God IS truth. It would be incorrect for me to say that God speaks truth. This would imply that He learned a truth that He now conveys to us. That is just not how that happens. God didn't learn truth; God IS truth. Therefore, anything that proceeds from His mouth just IS. So when God tells us in His word that we are His children, it IS truth. Even if you don't feel like you are a child of God, you are because He said you are!

That means we should learn to act like it! All too often, Christians live like they have been defeated by the world, but the truth is actually the opposite. God has already defeated this world. First of all, God the Father created all of it. Then God the Son, Jesus, redeemed or bought forgiveness for all of it. Then as if the first two weren't enough, God the Holy Spirit indwells all of it! So if you are a child of this Creator, Redeemer, Indweller God, how could you possibly be defeated? The answer is, you can't. Even if you feel defeated because of what you have done. You may be defeated in the perspective of your mind and attitude, but not in the reality of God's love, Jesus' forgiveness, and the Holy Spirit's indwelling. You just haven't yet learned how to walk in the victory you have been given.

So the Apostle goes on ...

"And what we will be has not yet been made known."

This is actually a glorious phrase. The writers in the Pulpit Commentary put it this way: "Our present state is known; our future remains still unrevealed.... we are in doubt about the construction" (Spence and Exell 1950, p. 71). This is entirely true. Who we are is not in question. God has answered that. It is who we will become that worries us. Because we have always felt defeated, we worry that we will amount to very little. That just doesn't need to be the case. We are not the helpless, hapless losers we see when we look in the mirror. We are, by declaration of God Himself, children of the King. Not paupers. Not losers. Not wimps. Not slaves to sin. We are children of the King! What we need to do is begin the process of acting like it.

Let me make a suggestion here that will be helpful the rest of the way through this epistle. Becoming the man or woman God says we are is a process. It is not an event. There is not going to be some shining moment when warm light flows down out of heaven and miraculously transforms us from sinner to saint. No. The actual transformation took part when you received forgiveness from Jesus. This allowed God the Father to declare you His child and allowed God the Holy Spirit to come into your life and begin to direct your actions. Now, here is the problem, you have to listen to the Holy Spirit as He guides you! Up to this point, you have been listening to your urges. Your urge to be angry, overeat, curse, drink, take drugs, go to places you don't belong, sleep with people to whom you don't belong, and many other urges have been the norm in your life. The sound of their call is familiar, even comforting.

Now there is a new voice! It is the voice of the Holy Spirit. This voice is known but not familiar ... yet. It is right but not always comforting ... yet. Therefore, you must do the WORK, and it is work, of training yourself to listen to this new voice. You will fail along the way. In fact, early on you will fail a lot. When you do, the old voices of your urges begin to scream at you and call you a failure. They remind you of every slip-up and say that you are still the loser you always thought you were. Remember, those voices are only crying out for their own survival! Those voices know that if you learn to listen to and surrender to the Holy Spirit of God, they are done. And so they fight. They scream. They scratch and claw at your insides until you can almost physically feel the battle. And in the midst of all that noise ... you need to hear ... and heed the Holy Spirit!

"But we know that when Christ appears, we shall be like him, for we shall see him as he is. All who have this hope in him purify themselves, just as he is pure."

It is in this process of purification, learning to hear and heed the Holy Spirit, that we are ultimately changed into the likeness of Christ. We learn to act like Him, think like Him, love like Him, and we learn to actually see Him.

Think about something. Have you ever seen light? I mean ... when you flip the switch on at home, do you see light? The answer is really no. You don't necessarily see the light. You see the effect of the light on everything around you. It is the light that lets you see the obstacles in your way. It is the light that lets you see the beauty in your world. It is the light that lets you see everything else, but you don't necessarily see the light itself.

"God is light," and while we see the effect of His presence on everything around us, we don't necessarily see Him until we get to know Him. The more know Christ, the more we see Christ. The more we see Christ, the more we actually begin to understand the God whose influence has illuminated everything around us. He has revealed the beauty within us, which is the beauty He put there but we haven't seen until now.

When I was a child, the family traveled to a place where we toured some underground caverns. I remember being awestruck by the beauty and majesty of the rock formations brought about by the work of water and gravity over the course of centuries. At one point on the tour, the guide got us to stand still and warned us, "Don't move." He then turned out the lights. A second ago, I was awestruck by the beauty that surrounded me; I had never seen anything like it and it was wonderful. Now, it was dark, and I mean completely dark. I literally placed my hand right in front of my face and I could not see even the faintest of outlines. I knew what my hand looked like and I knew it was there. I knew that cavern was beautiful and I knew all of it was there. I knew I came in here with my mom and dad and I knew they were still there. But I couldn't see anything. It was terrifying. I still remember restraining myself from screaming out for someone to turn on the lights!! Everything that was beautiful, comfortable, secure, and loving was hidden, somewhere in the darkness. And I was completely alone.

That experience only lasted a few seconds. Then they turned on the lights and there stood my mom and dad, my sister, and the stunning beauty of the cavern, but I wanted out as fast as possible. Although I didn't really understand it at the moment, let me tell you why I don't really like caves and caverns to this day. The light in there is dependent on humans for its ability to shine, and that is just too fragile. I wanted to get outside, because the light outside was from God. No human was able to turn that off.

Herein lies the difference between walking in the light of human wisdom and all of your urges to walking in the light of God's presence, *"for we shall see him as he is."* The reason that *"all who have this hope in him purify themselves, just as he is pure"* is because those who have come to know Him realize that everything but Him is fragile and prone to darkness. When we get to know Him, become more like Him, surrender our urges to Him, and learn the discipline of listening to His Holy Spirit, then the fragility and tendency to darkness of our prior life gives way to the eternal strength and light of His presence, His truth, His reality, His hope, and His love. *"Dear friends, now we are children of God."* Now, let's learn to act like it!

Day 3

"Everyone who sins breaks the law; in fact, sin is lawlessness. But you know that he appeared so that he might take away our sins. And in him is no sin. No one who lives in him keeps on sinning. No one who continues to sin has either seen him or known him. Dear children, do not let anyone lead you astray. The one who does what is right is righteous, just as he is righteous. The one who does what is sinful is of the devil, because the devil has been sinning from the beginning. The reason the Son of God appeared was to destroy the devil's work. No one who is born of God will continue to sin, because God's seed remains in them; they cannot go on sinning, because they have been born of God." (1 John 3:4-9)

Let me take this section of scripture and explain it in four stages that will help us unpack what the Apostle is saying here.

The Problem – *"Sin is lawlessness."*

The problem is sin. While today's culture complains about all of the problems in our society, they always ignore the real issue. At the risk of seeming overly simplistic and ticking people off, let me be clear: The problem was and is always sin.

The problem is not poverty. Poverty is caused by sin. Whether it is the sinfulness of a parent who refuses to care for the financial needs of their children, the sinfulness of an addict who spends lunch money on booze, the sinfulness of a landlord that is price gouging an uneducated family, or the sinfulness of a boss who is too greedy to pay a living wage ... the problem is actually sin.

But we can't talk about that. It might offend someone.

The problem is not the spiritual institution of marriage. The problem is sin. Whether it is the selfishness of a spouse who violates or simply rejects the marriage covenant, or the sinfulness of an abuser who insists on taking his or her anger out on a defenseless spouse ... the problem is sin.

But we can't talk about that. It might offend someone.

The problem is not our political systems. The problem is sin. Whether it is the greediness of government officials who steal monies given for the betterment of their people to enrich themselves, the government officials refuse to help anyone who won't bribe them, or the constant pattern of lies that accompany so many political campaigns ... the problem is sin.

In your life, sin is the problem as well. Sin is lawlessness and therefore creates a dangerous and unstable reality that most often leads to injury, destruction, addiction, or even death. As we said before, sin is a willful transgression of a known law. Sin is something you choose to do on purpose. The choice toward sin, the problem, is a choice away from Christ, the solution.

The Lifestyle – *"But you know that he appeared so that he might take away our sins. And in him is no sin. No one who lives in him keeps on sinning. No one who continues to sin has either seen him or known him."*

When we give in to sin once or twice, we begin to set a pattern of sinfulness; therefore, if sin is lawlessness, we begin a pattern of lawlessness. The truth is that our choices really matter. If we are going to be a follower of Christ, then we should follow Christ in our actions and choices. We should remember that *"no one,"* at least no one who is serious about being a Christian, *"keeps on sinning."* In fact, *"no one who continues to sin has either seen him or known him."* The reason for this is simple: *"And in Him is no sin."* So if I am going to emulate the one who has no sin, I cannot do that by living in consistent patterns of sinful behavior. Read what the commentators have to say as they speak of this verse: "The fact of the man's sinning proves that his perception and knowledge have been imperfect, if not superficial, or even imaginary; just as the fact of Christians leaving the Church proves that they never were really members of it (1 John 2:19)" (Spence and Exell 1950, p. 72).

Now I don't want anyone running around worrying that every little thing they do wrong causes them to be cast out of the church or proves that they were never part of the church in the first place. This teaching from the Apostle John is not intended to cause insecurity in our faith. God is not looking to throw you out; He is looking to keep you in. In the phrase, *"keeps on sinning,"* it is "clear that the word translated 'committeth' [keeps on] sin is literally 'doeth' sin, meaning one who lives continually and habitually in sin" (McGee 1983, p. 788). So what we need to address is less about an individual moment of failure and more about a habitual pattern of lawlessness. When we fall into a lifestyle of sin, we risk the very grace in which we find our hope.

The Mindset — *"Dear children, do not let anyone lead you astray. The one who does what is right is righteous, just as he is righteous. The one who does what is sinful is of the devil, because the devil has been sinning from the beginning. The reason the Son of God appeared was to destroy the devil's work."*

Let me say once again that our culture consistently leads us in the wrong direction. Many, if not most, in our society would be offended at the very suggestion that they have ever done anything sinful. So in order to sooth their oddly aching conscience, they explain away the sinfulness of sin. Then they work to *"lead you astray"* into their belief that God's word does not contain truth and should not be allowed to affect your day-to-day choices. They would just have you do what feels good and not worry one bit about God's law, which leads to lawlessness (sinfulness).

You must surrender your thinking to the guidance of the Holy Spirit that God has placed in you. Your lifestyle must be directed by the power of the Holy Spirit, because *"the one who does what is right is righteous, just as he is righteous."*

The Solution – *"No one who is born of God will continue to sin, because God's seed remains in them; they cannot go on sinning, because they have been born of God."*

Again, here we are talking about habitual patterns of sinfulness. There is no one who has completely and perfectly overcome sin. Every one of us falls, fails, and messes up sometimes, but we DO NOT have to live in a constant pattern of falls, fails, and messes. We can live free because we are *"born of God."* It is not our awesomeness that lets us live better; it is His grace, His love, and His indwelling. We can choose order or lawlessness, grace or sinfulness, life or death, God or Satan, and right or wrong.

Trust me ... choose God!

Day 4

"This is how we know who the children of God are and who the children of the devil are: Anyone who does not do what is right is not God's child, nor is anyone who does not love their brother and sister. For this is the message you heard from the beginning: We should love one another. Do not be like Cain, who belonged to the evil one and murdered his brother. And why did he murder him? Because his own actions were evil and his brother's were righteous." (1 John 3:10-12)

Lack of Love Leads to Lost-ness – *"This is how we know who the children of God are."*

You know there is a test to find out to whom someone belongs. I am not talking about a DNA test. While those are effective, they often are not necessary. When I was 18 months old, my dad chose to leave my mother, sister, and me. My mom then took my sister and me and moved from Florida, where I was born, back to North Carolina. She raised us there with the help of her sister, and ultimately married my step-dad who also helped raise us. I don't remember meeting my biological father until I was about six or seven years old. After that, I only saw him once a year, at most, my entire life. So this man did not raise me. In fact, there were dozens of adults who I knew better and was more influenced by than him. However, once I was a grown man, I began to realize something. Amazingly, I was like this man who had not raised me. We look alike, we act alike, we talk alike, and we even walk alike. None of this can be attributed to environment because I was never around him.

But we don't think alike.

I think like my mom and step-dad. I process right and wrong like they do. I may look and sound a lot like my biological father, but that is just genetics. When I make choices, I use a set of norms that were instilled in me by parenting, not by genetics. While it is true that you would not need a DNA test to say that my biological dad is my dad, you also would not find it difficult to figure out where I got my way of thinking. No DNA test required.

This is how it works with our spiritual life. It is clear that we were born children of sin. It doesn't take long for the selfishness, greed, pride, and weakness against wrongness to show. Our tendency toward doing what we should not do is legendary. We clearly are children of this world, but our God is trying to take what we were born with and redeem it. He is attempting to infiltrate our thinking and the way we process right and wrong. He is doing that by indwelling our lives. He is living with us. Very few of us have parents who planned out with intentionality what they wanted teach us about right and wrong. Very few, experienced parents have given written plans with predetermined markers for developmental achievement in the household. No, we just lived with them. We learned how to process right and wrong by watching them process right and wrong. We learned to be good by watching them be good. Then, when we are adults, we obviously resemble our parents, not just genetically but morally. The same happens when we surrender our time and temperament to Christ. As we spend more time with Him, the more He changes us. Ultimately, while we are still children of sin, there is something more. There is the residual effect of the forgiveness of the blood of Christ, the presence of the Holy Spirit, and the power of God the Father. The influence of God on our lives takes what we were born with and makes it better!

When we reject the forgiveness of Christ, the presence of the Spirit, and the power of the Father, we leave ourselves to the mercy of our sin-scarred starting point. And there is no mercy there. There is only failure, sin, brokenness, and lost-ness. The markers are really simple to see: *"Anyone who does not do what is right is not God's child, nor is anyone who does not love their brother and sister."* Such a person is truly lost.

Lack of Love Leads to Lawlessness – *"Do not be like Cain, who belonged to the evil one."*

There is a cost associated with a habitual pattern of giving in to the sinful desires in our lives. I have said it so many times. Sin is perfectly designed to bring destruction and death, yet it is so simple to fall into this sin that would kill us. The Apostle warns us here about not being like Cain. Cain is the oldest son of Adam and Eve. He is born to the original parents of mankind. Soon after his birth came the birth of his brother, Abel. Their story is recorded in Genesis, chapter 4. Both boys are the product of God-fearing parents. It seems clear from the story that Adam and Eve have taught the boys how to offer sacrifices to God and how to properly worship Him. Both boys do offer sacrifices. The Bible says this about their sacrifices:

> *Now Abel kept flocks, and Cain worked the soil. In the course of time Cain brought some of the fruits of the soil as an offering to the LORD. And Abel also brought an offering—fat portions from some of the firstborn of his flock. The LORD looked with favor on Abel and his offering, but on Cain and his offering he did not look with favor. So Cain was very angry, and his face was downcast. (Genesis 4:2-5)*

Now, at first, it seems that God just kind-of chose to like Abel better than Cain, but that just wasn't the case. We have to assume that Adam and Eve taught the boys about God's expectations. They would know them well since they used to take long walks with God in the garden (Genesis 3:8). From later Mosaic Law, we know that God always required an offering from the *"firstfruits"* or *"firstborn"* of whatever it is you were producing. Further, we know that only the very best should be offered to God as a sacrifice. Now look at this verse again. Cain brought *"some of the fruits"* of his work to God *"in the course of time."* Abel brought *"fat portions from some of the firstborn of his flock."* Cain brought what Cain wanted to give. Abel brought what God wanted to receive. Cain just wanted to fulfill the requirement while Abel wanted to worship

God. The difference is clear. Abel is striving to live a life of lawfulness while Cain is trying to hide a life of lawlessness. When God called him on it, Cain got mad! So mad, in fact, that he *"murdered his brother."* Why? *"Because his own actions were evil and his brother's were righteous."*

Listen, sinfulness, which leads to lawlessness, will cause you to do things you thought you would never do. It will cause you to stoop to lows you would have never considered before giving in to its destructive grip. It will cause you to hate people you were born to love. Sinfulness can ultimately lead you to the place where you are nothing more than someone who belongs *"to the evil one."* Don't take that path. Don't choose the path of Cain. Choose love. Choose righteousness. Choose life.

Day 5

"Do not be surprised, my brothers and sisters, if the world hates you. We know that we have passed from death to life, because we love each other. Anyone who does not love remains in death. Anyone who hates a brother or sister is a murderer, and you know that no murderer has eternal life residing in him." (1 John 3:13-15)

The World Hates — *"Do not be surprised, my brothers and sisters, if the world hates you."*

When others are surprised with the world acting like the world, it surprises me. The world is going to hate you because it already hated your Savior, Jesus Christ. *"If the world hates you, keep in mind that it hated me first. If you belonged to the world, it would love you as its own. As it is, you do not belong to the world, but I have chosen you out of the world. That is why the world hates you"* (John 15:18-19). We need to remember that this hatred comes in many different forms. Sometimes it is outward and angry. Sometimes people will literally insult you or even threaten you because of your faith in Christ.

One weekend when Tina and I were in college majoring in Music, we were preparing to go to a church and sing for them about the Christ we serve. One of the other students asked us what we were preparing to do and so we told him. He was really offended and said: "Why would you use the art of music to perpetuate that kind of fantasy?" Well, I was pretty young and not really sure how to answer him. So in my ignorance, the Holy Spirit let me do the right thing and ignore him. That was the first time I came into contact with someone who was actually offended by my faith, but it wasn't the last.

Truth is that as long as the devil is out there, he is going to angrily fight against God's Church. He has been angry with God from the beginning. The Bible describes a war in heaven (Revelation 12:7-9) and clearly says that Lucifer, who is the angel that became Satan, wanted to take over God's throne (Isaiah 14:12-15). And in his defeat, Satan has found a hatred for God and His people that has never been quenched and causes problems to this day.

So, Satan hates.

And the world is largely under his influence. So the world hates. Honestly, you don't have to look very hard to see that this is simply, and sadly, a very true statement.

The Church Loves – *"We know that we have passed from death to life, because we love each other."*

The mark of a true believer is the ability to love others even when they don't deserve it. Just as the world is marked and has learned to act like its father, the devil, we are marked and are learning to act like our Father, God. Again, this transformation in our lives is not an event. It is not some Hollywood style moment that occurs and ends with a happily ever after song. No, our transformation is a process. Don't get me wrong; I wish it were an event. I wish there was some magic spell that could be spoken over any individual that would just instantly change them in to a saint, but it doesn't work like that. We are on a life-long journey of passing *"from death to life."* The driving force behind our ability to accomplish that journey comes *"because we love each other."* Love is the key to finally finding a pathway to forgiveness. It is the key to finding hope. It is the key to standing with one another. It is the key part of being like Christ. The Bible tells us in one of the most well-known passages in scripture: *"God so loved the world that he gave his one and only Son, that whoever believes in him shall not perish but have eternal life"* (John 3:16). When we learn to act in love, we learn to act in godliness.

Love Versus Death – *"Anyone who does not love remains in death. Anyone who hates a brother or sister is a murderer, and you know that no murderer has eternal life residing in him."*

Death is a state that religious people can easily exist. In Jesus' day, He constantly ran into people who were highly religious but who knew very little about God, His love, or His will. Speaking with one such group, He said to them: *"You belong to your father, the devil, and you want to carry out your father's desires. He was a murderer from the beginning, not holding to the truth, for there is no truth in him. When he lies, he speaks his native language, for he is a liar and the father of lies"* (John 8:44).

He clearly points out that the problem for this group of overly religious people is not that they don't know how to do religious things; it is that they don't know how to live like the God they say they are following. He goes on to say: *"Yet because I tell the truth, you do not believe me! Can any of you prove me guilty of sin? If I am telling the truth, why don't you believe me? Whoever belongs to God hears what God says. The reason you do not hear is that you do not belong to God"* (John 8:45-47).

Without love, we cannot know God. Without knowing God, we cannot find life. Without finding the life that God would give us, we are condemned to remain in death.

Day 6

"This is how we know what love is: Jesus Christ laid down his life for us. And we ought to lay down our lives for our brothers and sisters. If anyone has material possessions and sees a brother or sister in need but has no pity on them, how can the love of God be in that person? Dear children, let us not love with words or speech but with actions and in truth." (1 John 3:16-18)

Once we experience the love of Christ for us, the natural response should be to give that love out to others. There always are people around us who just need to know that someone cares. They are hurting and no one even knows it. A simple show of God's love can make a world of a difference. Although there are many reasons that we should show the love of Christ to the world around us, let's look specifically at two we find right here.

Love not only defines us, but it is also defined by Christ our Savior.

"This is how we know what love is: Jesus Christ laid down his life for us."

Jesus defines love. Jesus embodies love. Jesus displayed love. Jesus is our example. Sometimes people seem to think that they have love all figured out. They seem to believe that they can explain the science of love, the psychology of love, or the mechanics of love. Let me assure you that they cannot. In fact, they are normally not talking about love at all. They are talking about an overwhelming feeling. Those who talk about the science of love are talking about the chemicals that collide or combine in our bodies to generate a certain feeling of euphoria or warmth. Now while that feeling is really awesome, it isn't love. Those who talk about the psychology of love talk about the emotions that develop toward one person or another and how those emotions can be nurtured, destroyed, built up, or eliminated. Although this is really helpful information, it isn't love. Those who talk about the mechanics of love are most often just manipulators who believe they have figured out how to make people believe things are not actually real. And that definitely is not love.

Love is not a feeling. Feelings come and go. True love stays. Love is more than just an emotional connection, because those, too, come and go. Love is definitely not manipulative. Love is more. Love is a choice, a decision. It is an act of the will. Many people may think that just takes all the romance out of love, but it doesn't. Think it through. Feeling-based love is limited to the endurance of feelings. Emotion-based love is limited to the duration of emotions. Manipulative love is really not about the one being loved at all. When love is a choice, it can endure. It has the power to be more.

Jesus defines love by His actions. If we are to take this verse seriously, then love is sacrificial. Love is all about the other person. Love is about what sets the other person free, not what serves me. That kind of sacrificial, others-centered love is not possible if it is based on feelings, emotions, or manipulation. It requires a selflessness that can only be found in Christ.

Love not only serves us, but it also drives us to serve.

Real love serves. It serves for the sake of service. Real love is not someone who is serving just to get a tip or gain some other favor. If you are serving someone just to earn some points or accomplish a larger goal, then that isn't love at all; that is selfishness. When we love like Christ, we serve for the sake of being like Him. It is interesting to consider how much of the world's problems could be settled through real love for others. Just take the list we used earlier. Poverty would not be able to exist if we all operated out of love for one another. Marriages would be peaceful and happy places if we all operated out of love for one another. Governmental structures would actually protect and serve without power trips or greed if we all operated out of love for one another. Now, I know we live in a fallen world and what I am describing is just not possible when we are so broken and driven by sin instead of love.

God's people, followers of Christ, should be different.

What if we actually learned to *"not love with words or speech but with actions and in truth"*? We could make a huge difference, even in moments that we didn't know the need existed.

Just recently, my wife and I took a singing group from our church university out to eat. We took them to a restaurant that we regularly visit. We were familiar with the waitress to the point that she actually knew my order before I said it! Well, she did a wonderful job keeping up with the 18 folks we had at the table. When the meal was over, the university students all lined up to sing for her (common practice for them). They had a fun song that they had made up and they would sing it to anyone who served them along their travels. The waitress, seeing them line up, assumed they wanted her to take a picture of them. "No, we want to sing to you," they said and began to sing. As they sang their thanks for her service, she began to cry. "It's my last day on this job," she told us through her tears. She was moving away for family reasons and was sad about leaving the area. And there they were. Those kids must have sounded like an angel choir affirming that young lady's work and efforts on a very difficult day. That's just how God works ... if you let Him.

Will you let Him?

Day 7

"This is how we know that we belong to the truth and how we set our hearts at rest in his presence: If our hearts condemn us, we know that God is greater than our hearts, and he knows everything. Dear friends, if our hearts do not condemn us, we have confidence before God and receive from him anything we ask, because we keep his commands and do what pleases him. And this is his command: to believe in the name of his Son, Jesus Christ, and to love one another as he commanded us. The one who keeps God's commands lives in him, and he in them. And this is how we know that he lives in us: We know it by the Spirit he gave us." (1 John 3:19-24)

A Heart at Work is a Heart at Rest!

"This is how we know that we belong to the truth and how we set our hearts at rest in his presence…. And this is his command: to believe in the name of his Son, Jesus Christ, and to love one another as he commanded us. The one who keeps God's commands lives in him, and he in them."

So many times people ask me, "Pastor, how do I know I am saved? I am just worried that I am not really a child of God." Many of those folks have something in common. They spend a lot of time THINKING about God and salvation. They spend their time reading and studying and sometimes arguing on some blog. All of that time wondering leaves them … wondering. You know who rarely asks me that question. People who spend a lot of time WORKING for God and His salvation of others. Doing what God has called us to do is a far superior way of assuring ourselves that we are children of God. When you spend all of your time thinking about it and not doing anything about it, you just confuse yourself. I have been through a lot of classes in my lifetime, and I have sat with some really highly educated people. Most of them have been wonderful teachers, and I have thanked God for all they have invested in me. However, a few have left me convinced that they had studied their field for so long without practicing it that they had confused themselves. Their theoretical hypotheses were bound to lead to empty results. Sometimes, unintentionally, a Christian can do that. The Apostle John says it right here. A simple three-step process to be lived out and repeated on a daily basis:

1. Believe in Jesus

2. Love one another

3. Keep God's commands

If you can stay busy DOING these three things, you will find that you have less time for WORRYING about other things.

God's Peace

"If our hearts condemn us, we know that God is greater than our hearts, and he knows everything."

Sometimes even those who are working hard in the faith are left with doubts. In those moments, the devil can whisper to us reminders of every failure, every attitude, and every thought that we have somehow allowed to get out of God's perfect will. Once he has us thinking about all of our failures, he will start having us question all of our work. Was it worth it? Has it accomplished anything? Was it really what God wanted? Suddenly, even the most active believers are riddled with doubt.

In those moments, remember these words: *"God is greater than our hearts, and he knows everything."* This Greek word translated as *"hearts"* is the word *kardia,* which obviously means the organ that pumps blood through our bodies. In Greek, much like in English, this word takes on a deeper meaning: "The centre and seat of spiritual life" (Blue Letter Bible). In other words, when our center of spiritual understanding is off, we must trust the declaration of God that we are His so that we can fight off the confusion that is being brought in by the enemy of our souls. Here's some encouragement we find in Romans:

"If you declare with your mouth, 'Jesus is Lord,' and believe in your heart that God raised him from the dead, you will be saved." (Romans 10:9)

"Therefore, there is now no condemnation for those who are in Christ Jesus." (Romans 8:1)

"Who shall separate us from the love of Christ? Shall trouble or hardship or persecution or famine or nakedness or danger or sword?... No, in all these things we are more than conquerors

through him who loved us. For I am convinced that neither death nor life, neither angels nor demons, neither the present nor the future, nor any powers, neither height nor depth, nor anything else in all creation, will be able to separate us from the love of God that is in Christ Jesus our Lord." (Romans 8:35-39)

God's Power

"Dear friends, if our hearts do not condemn us, we have confidence before God and receive from him anything we ask, because we keep his commands and do what pleases him."

In the same way that we feel a bit lost and discouraged when our hearts try to condemn us, we sense the absolute power of God when our hearts do not condemn us! These are the great moments of the Christian walk: moments when our work and our faith fall into sync. In these moments, we are working and trusting. We are fighting and resting. We are moving and waiting.

We work with all of our might because we are convinced of God's great plan for our lives. We strive because we see progress and want to accomplish all that God will allow. Our work is fully based in trust that God is empowering every step of our journey!

We fight to defend the powerful movement of God in our lives. We recognize that these moments are special and should be nurtured and protected. We rest in knowing that the ultimate arbiter of our effectiveness is God, and we can trust Him.

We move because there is no better time to move faster than when you are already moving freely. There is no stopping when you really get going! And so we move while listening and watching for the Holy Spirit of God to show us our next turn. His direction is our singular goal.

When our will and God's will are in sync, we *"receive from him anything we ask, because we keep his commands and do what pleases him."*

WEEK

4

Day 1

"Dear friends, do not believe every spirit, but test the spirits to see whether they are from God, because many false prophets have gone out into the world. This is how you can recognize the Spirit of God: Every spirit that acknowledges that Jesus Christ has come in the flesh is from God, but every spirit that does not acknowledge Jesus is not from God. This is the spirit of the antichrist, which you have heard is coming and even now is already in the world." (1 John 4:1-3)

You have to be careful whom you listen to these days!!

I don't know if you have noticed, but there is a trend in our culture that is quite disturbing to me. It seems that today's culture insists that every opinion be given an equal level of standing in any discussion at any time. While that may seem fair to you, it's really not a very smart or fair way to think. All opinions are not created equal! To take this new philosophy of fairness to the extreme, those who are either ignorant or not stable with sound mind to give an opinion is treated with the same weight of those who are educated and balanced. While this alone may seem to just promote politeness, it gets out-of-hand when people who want to skew the actual understanding of events simply lie. Instead, they falsely create an entirely new story. They proceed to offer that story as their opinion and expect to be given the same level of respect as anyone telling the truth. It doesn't matter that their version of events is demonstrably untrue. In striving for fairness, we lose any hope of resolution, understanding, growth, or accuracy. It really is crazy!

And it exists in the Church! Today, many people will read the Bible without any attempt to actually understand what it says. Instead, they read the Bible in a blatant attempt to make it say what they want it to say, and they ignore or even try to alter its content! This is the very type of scenario that the Apostle John is facing in the culture of his day. This baby church is facing people who want to twist the teachings of Jesus and His disciples for their own gain. The main group, as we spoke of earlier, is the Gnostics. They argued that Jesus was not really God in the flesh. Instead, they wanted everyone to believe that they had some special connection with God that made them smarter and wiser than everyone else. This gave them power over anyone who chose to follow them since the voice of God could only be understood by one of these Gnostic leaders. The Apostle rightly calls these people *"false prophets."* He warns his first-century church to be on the lookout for these people because they will be led astray if they follow them. Simply put, the Apostle John is battling to maintain the true teaching and history of Jesus who IS the Christ. He gives this early church a simple test for finding out if someone is speaking truth. This test is still useful for us today.

"This is how you can recognize the Spirit of God: Every spirit that acknowledges that Jesus Christ has come in the flesh is from God, but every spirit that does not acknowledge Jesus is not from God."

The test is really simple. When listening to someone teach or express an opinion about a biblical matter, simply ask yourself, "Is what I am hearing keeping with what I would expect to hear from Jesus?" There are a couple of catchwords here that really do tend to set the true believer apart from the non-believer. If the following four words can be agreed to, then you have found someone in which you can share common ground, even if you do not agree on every point.

This is Jesus – The historical person who walked the streets of Jerusalem and other villages and towns in Israel approximately 2,000 years ago. Jesus is the historical person whose life story is told in the Gospels of Matthew, Mark, Luke, and John. Jesus is the historical person whose teachings we have been given and is explained in the remainder of the New Testament.

This is Christ – the Greek word here is *Christos* and literally translated means the anointed one (Blue Letter Bible). This is the one whom the Jews have been waiting for and the one promised to be anointed by God to deliver His people from bondage. Using the title Christ after the name Jesus clearly states that you believe Jesus is the one who was promised to be the hope of the world.

This is Flesh – Now here is one half of a real dilemma. You see the Gnostics of John's day did not believe that anything good came from anything material or non-spiritual. They thought that all physical matter was evil, and that our deliverance from evil would only come through our passing out of this physical world and entering into a spiritual one. To them, the idea of the Christ being a physical person was insulting! They taught that the spirit of Christ indwelled Jesus and left just before he died. This clearly is not what the Apostles taught. When John gives us this test, he intentionally places the humanity of Jesus in the test. Jesus is 100% human, so He understands us. He gets us because He has been there.

This is God – Here is the other half of that dilemma. Some would argue that Jesus wasn't God at all. For them, Jesus is just a great moral teacher and nothing more. These folks would accept what Jesus had to say as some good ideas, but not as eternal truth from the mouth of God. The Greek word here is *Theos*, which means God (Blue Letter Bible). So the Apostle wants us to clearly look for people who will openly declare that Jesus is God. 100% human AND 100% God.

The simple test is set in place, and it still works today. I have met people throughout my ministry that would deny one or more of the distinctions that the Apostle John listed as absolutes. I have even met pastors who would not be able to pass this simple test. They preach every Sunday from pulpits and yet fail to believe in Jesus as a real historical figure, or that He is the Christ, or a human being, or that He is God incarnate (in the flesh). These people should not be mistreated or spoken to rudely, but they should be understood for what they are: *"This is the spirit of the antichrist, which you have heard is coming and even now is already in the world."* There is plenty of this *"spirit of the antichrist"* in our world today. Sometimes we are so busy looking for the Hollywood generated version of some slick golden boy who is the antichrist that we fail to recognize and therefore protect against the thousands who speak, teach, and carry the *"spirit of the antichrist"* to the culture around us.

Let the Apostle remind you, *"Dear friends, do not believe every spirit, but test the spirits to see whether they are from God, because many false prophets have gone out into the world."*

Day 2

"You, dear children, are from God and have overcome them, because the one who is in you is greater than the one who is in the world." (1 John 4:4)

The Apostle John speaks with his *"dear children"* and sets the unseen parameters of the spiritual and theological battle. He does this to define the person and work of Jesus that is occurring at the time. To this band of believers, the odds must have seemed stacked against them. How were they supposed to get proper teaching and understanding to their people in order to counter this false teaching? There was no Internet, phone system, TV, radio, or mail service. There was nothing but men who could travel from town to town. And there were a lot of towns! There was one weapon that the Apostle John wanted his people to remember.

The Holy Spirit

It was true that the Apostle was facing an almost impossible task of training people who were hearing the Gospel for the first time. It was true that he had to somehow come against *"false prophets"* and the *"spirit of the antichrist"* at every turn and in every town. The truth of Christ was in jeopardy of being watered down or even lost altogether. It also was true that the Holy Spirit was living inside every one of those first-century believers, and the Holy Spirit could do what the Apostle John could not!

It always amazes me when I think of the formation of the early church. The growth of Christianity was so sudden and rapid in those first couple of centuries. There was no real technology to help them stay connected or help them formulate the way each separate church thought or taught. However, the Gospel of Christ still remained intact. How is that even possible? The only answer is a God answer. God, the Holy Spirit living inside of each believer, fought for and defended the faith and understanding of each one. Even though it looked like there was no way for this early church that was so spread out, so disconnected, so rapidly expanding to hold it all together, God was going to do just that! It looked like they could not win, but in reality, they had already won! *"You, dear children, are from God and have overcome them."* The Apostle's words here are spoken in past tense. This means that the work was already done! The victory was already won. The world would have said that such an accomplishment was absolutely impossible. The Holy Spirit said it was already done!

You know, it still works this way today. So often as Christians, we feel defeated. We look at our culture and feel defeated. We look at our communities and feel defeated. We look at our lives and feel defeated. I agree with the Apostle John on this one! Not only are we not defeated but also our victory has already been won. How many times have we heard the testimony of someone who has found victory in God? I have stood and spoken with addicts who knew they were defeated by the drug that the world had brought into their lives, but then the Holy Spirit shows up and changes it all. I have spoken with couples whose marriage was on the rocks and their family crumbling, but then the Holy Spirit shows up and changes it all. I have spoken with people whose finances were in deep trouble, but then the Holy Spirit shows up and changes it all.

God changes everything!

Let me explain how this works.

God is all-powerful – Your Father is greater than your problem!

There is nothing that our Father cannot do. He created it all and He knows how it all works. With nothing more than a word from His lips, entire galaxies are formed and brought into being. *"See what great love the Father has lavished on us, that we should be called children of God!"* (1 John 3:1). This means that your Father is already greater than your problem!

God is all-loving – Your Savior has already forgiven your faults!

Jesus, your Savior, has already taken care of all the guilt and shame that overwhelms you. Oftentimes, we face seemingly insurmountable problems that are entirely of our own making. In moments like these, we feel defeated and guilty, but the guilt is no longer ours to carry! Jesus has already taken that guilt and forgiven us. That was the whole point of the cross. He took on crucifixion for you so that you would not need to crucify yourself! So stop doing it! Stop punishing yourself for the very things for which Christ has already forgiven. Stop with the guilt and get on with the living!

God is in you – Your life is filled with the Holy Spirit!

Now, let's review. God the Father is bigger than all of your problems. Jesus the Son, our Savior, has paid the price for all of your failures. Now God the Holy Spirit has moved into your life. He can empower you, deliver you, guide you, and walk with you. Christianity is not like so many other religions where you are just given some guidelines and then left on your own to figure out how to follow them. And thank God it isn't like that! In those religions, only a few people are smart enough, strong enough, or committed enough to actually see it through. Often even they need to climb some mountain and get away from the world, becoming some kind of monk in a monastery in order to really live it out. They run away from the world in order to be "holy."

We don't need to run away; we have already overcome the world!

Listen again to the Apostle's words here and memorize them: *"The one who is in you is greater than the one who is in the world."*

Write that down somewhere. Post it on a wall. Put it on the mirror that you use every morning or night. Put these words anywhere you will see it every day, because they are true. This world is bigger than you and, in many ways, has defeated you. But now ... empowered by the Father ... forgiven by the Savior ... and indwelt by the Holy Spirit ... you are more! The world is no match for what God has made you. One more time, read it, hear it, believe it, and live it!

"You, dear children, are from God and have overcome them, because the one who is in you is greater than the one who is in the world."

Day 3

"They are from the world and therefore speak from the viewpoint of the world, and the world listens to them. We are from God, and whoever knows God listens to us; but whoever is not from God does not listen to us. This is how we recognize the Spirit of truth and the spirit of falsehood." (1 John 4:5-6)

Listen to the way Jesus says something very similar during his ministry here on earth: *"If the world hates you, keep in mind that it hated me first. If you belonged to the world, it would love you as its own. As it is, you do not belong to the world, but I have chosen you out of the world. That is why the world hates you"* (John 15:18-19). It really should not surprise us that the unbelieving world would not want to hear us speak of a God and a salvation that they are convinced they do not need or want.

The term *"the world"* is the Greek word *kosmos* and has various meanings. The one I think the Apostle is referring to here is "the ungodly multitude; the whole mass of men alienated from God, and therefore hostile to the cause of Christ" (Blue Letter Bible). We cannot deny that we know people like this. People like this have always surrounded the church. Again, He says to His disciples, *"If the world hates you, keep in mind that it hated me first."* And so this struggle between the ungodly world and the people of God continues to rage today.

The question is not whether the battle is real; the question is how will you and I respond?

Sometimes Christians respond to a hostile world with amazement or anger. These reactions are really not logical. When society ridicules our faith or the government passes laws that limit our faith, we need to remember that this is just the ungodly acting ungodly. They are just being themselves, and they are not alone. The Apostle reminds us that, *"They are from the world and therefore speak from the viewpoint of the world, and the world listens to them."* So they gather themselves together in large and small groups and reinforce their beliefs. They pool their collective lack of understanding of God and declare that they have somehow solved the problem or discovered that God is dead. This is not new. There is no reason for the Christian to be surprised by these actions. It has always been this way.

When we react with amazement or anger to those around us who are caught in worldly thinking, we actually do damage to the cause of Christ. Take for example, a family gathering. Within that family gathering, let's say there is someone who has married into the family and does not think like the rest of the family. Let's say that the rest of the family is Christian and has been raised in an environment where the word of God is taught and salvation has been accepted. Then enters this worldly person. He or she has been raised in an environment where the idea of God or the Bible is ridiculed and thought to be unintelligent or simplistic. That person is going to eventually say something that is offensive to the Gospel. Not always out of a mean spirit, but out of what has been taught and entrenched in his or her thinking. Well, likewise, one of the believers in the family is going to eventually say something that is offensive to the worldly views. Again, not necessarily out of a mean spiritedness, but out of what has been taught and entrenched in his or her thinking.

What is the difference between the two? Both have been insulted and offended, and both are acting out of what they are convinced is true. Both, we will assume, are sincere. The difference should be that the believer was expecting this and should react the same way Jesus always did ... in love.

Defend Truth

Jesus always defended truth. However, keep in mind that He saved His harshest defense of truth for the religious leaders who were misusing that truth. For the people of the world, Jesus, while still defending truth, shows a great deal of patience and compassion. In many churches today, there seems to be a belief that if you are not intentionally offensive when speaking God's truth, you cannot be effectively defending God's truth. This just isn't the case. In fact, being intentionally offensive has the opposite effect. These offensive people have learned and lived in a world where anger is the norm, and now they are currently living in a world where tolerance is the creed. In the setting of creedal tolerance, any idea, position, or statement regardless of its basis in truth or sanity must simply be greeted with a smile and a nod. Now, one who claims to be spiritual and know God is acting like a jerk. The heathen was polite, but the Christian was angry and defensive. In today's culture, that automatically makes the Christian wrong.

Deny Anger

Do not give anger a foothold in your conversation. The word of God has power that the teachings of this world do not have, and there is no need for you to try and assert that power in some angry outburst. A simple and calm presentation of the truth of scripture allows that truth to be heard. When truth is heard, it can take root and bring a change in thinking. The Apostle Paul puts it this way:

> *How, then, can they call on the one they have not believed in? And how can they believe in the one of whom they have not heard? And how can they hear without someone preaching to them? And how can anyone preach unless they are sent? As it is written: 'How beautiful are the feet of those who bring good news!' But not all the Israelites* [worldly unbelievers, in our case] *accepted the good news. For Isaiah says, 'Lord, who has believed our message?' Consequently, faith comes from hearing the message, and the message is heard through the word about Christ. (Romans 10:14-17)*

Display Love

"The message is heard through the word about Christ." It is also heard through the actions of Christ. It is not anger or sharp words that will win the world. It is not

passionate rhetoric that will win the world. It is not intelligence or a calculated debate that will win the world. It is not power, money, blessings, cursing, big new buildings, or fancy stage sets.

The world will be won over to the good news of Jesus Christ through love.

Day 4

"Dear friends, let us love one another, for love comes from God. Everyone who loves has been born of God and knows God. Whoever does not love does not know God, because God is love." (1 John 4:7-8)

Here the Apostle John begins a long section of teaching about love. John was known as *"the disciple whom Jesus loved"* (John 13:23). In his writings, he often talks about loving one another and loving God. Because of this, history has sometimes painted him as a bit of a wimp. Leonardo da Vinci, in The Last Supper, painted John with long, curly, reddish hair and a very feminine face. He was not alone in this type of depiction of John. The images are unfortunate. They have fostered a belief that lovingness is weakness, and the opposite is actually true. It takes strength to love. John had plenty of strength. Jesus described John and his brother, James, as the *"sons of thunder"* (Mark 3:17). This indicates that they were strong, forceful, loud, and direct in their speaking. This man was no wimp, and I can almost guarantee that he did not have a feminine face framed with flowing red curls.

Show Love to Know God

Showing love is not showing weakness. In fact, it is by showing love that we actually learn to know God. You just cannot know a person unless you know what drives them, what defines them, and what they're all about. God is all about love. The Apostle tells us

"God is love." Here we have a second working definition of God given to us by the Apostle John. He told us in chapter 1 that *"God is light"* and we should walk in that light. Now he tells us that *"God is love"* and we should walk in that love. We cannot walk in what we do not know. Therefore, if we are ever to actually know God, we must come to know love.

Know God Intellectually

In most languages, there are many words for love. English is not so functional on this point. We use this one word to say so many different things, and it sometimes gets confusing or downright awkward. When the Apostle John says, *"God is love,"* he uses the word *agape* (Blue Letter Bible). This particular word that we translate to *"love"* carries the connotation of unconditional love. In other words, God is unconditionally affectionate toward all people as a matter of His nature. He is a loving God, and His love is unconditional. This fact really matters if we are ever going to intellectually understand who God is and what God expects of us.

For instance, it would be incorrect to say that God chooses to sometimes show love. That would leave us believing that He could also choose to not show love. If God chooses to show love here but not there, then the God of the Bible would become little more than the ancient fickle gods of past cultures. Those gods were known to show love sometimes. They also were known to play games with humans or use humans to their own selfish ends. They were sometimes known to kill and destroy just to satisfy their own hunger for death, blood, and worship. But sometimes they chose to love.

Our God is not like that. He does not choose to love. He IS love. That means that there will never come a moment when the God of Heaven does not love you unconditionally. No other religion teaches about such a God. No other scriptures show that kind of consistent, unending, unconditional love from a Creator. Only in the Bible do you find this. To know God is to intellectually understand that love is His default setting and He will never violate that.

Know God Internally

Knowing in my mind that God is love and He will always act out in love is not the same thing as internalizing His love for me and everyone else. It is internalizing His love in such a way that we learn to live it out and, as a result, our lives are changed. God is love and He always loves unconditionally. We just aren't that good. While it is in God's nature to love, our nature has been damaged by sin. That sinful scar that has been left on our souls causes us to have a tendency to not love like God loves. While love may be God's default setting, our default setting is love for those who love us and anger, fear, hatred, or indifference to those who do not love us. Jesus said:

If you love those who love you, what credit is that to you? Even sinners love those who love them. And if you do good to those who are good to you, what credit is that to you? Even sinners do that.... But love your enemies, do good to them, and lend to them without expecting to get anything back. Then your reward will be great, and you will be children of the Most High, because he is kind to the ungrateful and wicked. Be merciful, just as your Father is merciful. (Luke 6:32-36)

You see it, right? While it is in God's nature to love unconditionally at all times, sin has damaged our nature to the point that such love is no longer natural. We have to try. We have to work at it. We have to struggle against anger, resentment, hatred, and fear. I think the most frightening thing about this is not, in fact, the anger, resentment, hatred, or fear. The most frightening thing is indifference. Furthermore, I think indifference is what society seems to be celebrating. The concept of tolerance is really a thinly veiled philosophy of indifference. Since society does not believe that we (humans) actually have the capacity to love people who are not like us, society will at least teach us not to hate, to just be indifferent, unmoved, and uncaring. Those might say: "Well, preacher, I don't really love many people, but that's OK because I don't really hate people either. I just leave them alone." That is perhaps the most frightening of all positions to take. What if God were indifferent toward us? What if He just didn't care? What a dark world that would be? Then someone might say: "Well, you may be all worked up about this love stuff preacher, but indifference has never killed anybody."

You are wrong. Just ask Nobel Peace Prize winner and Auschwitz survivor Elie Wiesel: "The opposite of love is not hate, it's indifference. The opposite of art is not ugliness, it's indifference. The opposite of faith is not heresy, it's indifference. And the opposite of life is not death, it's indifference" (Architects of Peace Foundation). It was indifference that allowed the slaughter of millions of Jews during World War II. Indifference is still killing today. From the starving children of impoverished nations, to sex trafficking, to the slaughter of Christians at the hands of radical Islamic regimes, to the completely preventable suicides of forgotten and lonely people in our own neighborhoods ... indifference kills.

But love ... God ... is never indifferent.

When we are indifferent to (do not love) those around us, we do *"not know God, because God is love."*

Day 5

"This is how God showed his love among us: He sent his one and only Son into the world that we might live through him. This is love: not that we loved God, but that he loved us and sent his Son as an atoning sacrifice for our sins. Dear friends, since God so loved us, we also ought to love one another. No one has ever seen God; but if we love one another, God lives in us and his love is made complete in us. This is how we know that we live in him and he in us: He has given us of his Spirit. And we have seen and testify that the Father has sent his Son to be the Savior of the world. If anyone acknowledges that Jesus is the Son of God, God lives in them and they in God." (1 John 4:9-15)

Show Love to Show God

If we are to show love in an effort to know God, then we must also show love in an effort to show God to the world around us. There is a central command within this set of verses: *"Dear friends, since God so loved us, we also ought to love one another."* Showing God's love is how we communicate God's presence and goodness throughout the world.

Go and Show

"This is how God showed his love among us: He sent his one and only Son into the world that we might live through him. This is love: not that we loved God, but that he loved us and sent his Son as an atoning sacrifice for our sins."

God did not simply sit in Heaven and have loving thoughts toward us. No, He came to us in order to show us His love. Honestly, since He is God and He is always in charge, He could have just continued to send His word down through priests and prophets. He really did not have to show up, but His love for us compelled Him to come to us. Humanity was hurting and lost. Humanity was trapped in sin, sorrow, sickness, and death. Humanity had no hope for an eternity any better than the struggle that was this life and this world. God, in His love for us, could fix all of that.

And He did.

God showed up. He came into our mess to be our Messiah. Now we are called to be like Him. That means we must do more than just sit in our comfortable homes and chairs and talk about how much we love the world. We must show up! We need to have an active love for those in need. If all we do is talk about it, we really are not accomplishing anything at all.

Know and Show

"No one has ever seen God; but if we love one another, God lives in us and his love is made complete in us."

How will anyone see a God they have never seen? How will they see a God they cannot see? How, in our physical world, will we help people see our spiritual God? The answer is simple. We have experienced Him. We know Him. We have seen His light and are walking in His light. Our God is more than just a concept or theology from a book. It is a real relationship that we have attained and fostered with the God of Heaven. The world does not have that relationship. How then will they ever see this wonderful God that we have seen and have come to know and love?

They will see Him through us. When the world looks at us and sees us looking up at God, it makes them look up. In other words, our lives draw attention to God. This is good news but it is also a warning. The good news is that our lives will automatically draw attention to God as long as we claim Him and let others know we believe in Him. The warning is the same. People are watching us. When we claim the presence of Christ in our lives, they are attributing our actions and attitudes to the God we say we serve. If those actions and attitudes are less than godly, then the people who are watching us get a skewed or incorrect concept of our God. This happens so often that many in our culture simply reject Christians without a second thought. They have been flooded with images of so-called Christians screaming angrily and holding signs that say "GOD HATES" whatever it is they are protesting. These images wound the Church and give entirely the wrong image of God. His love for people is unconditional, even when those people are living in open rebellion to God. And sometimes they aren't really living in open rebellion to the actual God of the Bible. They are living in open rebellion against the god they see in the angry, hateful voices of people who obviously do not know love and, therefore, cannot possibly know Him.

Live and Show

"This is how we know that we live in him and he in us: He has given us of his Spirit. And we have seen and testify that the Father has sent his Son to be the Savior of the world. If anyone acknowledges that Jesus is the Son of God, God lives in them and they in God. And so we know and rely on the love God has for us."

In the end, we need to *"live in him and he in us."* There is a wrong view of salvation that causes a great deal of trouble within the Church. Some say their actions have no bearing on their salvation. This is just bad theology. *"For it is by grace you have been saved, through faith—and this is not from yourselves, it is the gift of God—not by works, so that no one can boast"* (Ephesians 2:8-9). While no one can earn salvation, real salvation is going to come with a desire to *"live in him and he in us."* If we walk in this world the same way we did before knowing Christ, then what has effectively changed? The answer is nothing. When there is no change in the actions of the hands, one can be fairly certain that there has been no change in the attitudes of the heart.

The world needs to see the love of God lived out in our lives. It is important! It is more important than anything else we teach, do, say, or show. Because when they see us acting like Him, they tend to find Him. That is what every single human on this planet needs: A relationship with the God of the Bible who loves them unconditionally!

Day 6

"And so we know and rely on the love God has for us. God is love. Whoever lives in love lives in God, and God in them. This is how love is made complete among us so that we will have confidence on the day of judgment: In this world we are like Jesus. There is no fear in love. But perfect love drives out fear, because fear has to do with punishment. The one who fears is not made perfect in love." (1 John 4:16-18)

Show Love to Trust God

You know it matters what God we follow. All gods are not created equal. There really are only a few categories of world religions or beliefs about gods.

Polytheism – A Religion of Fate

Polytheism is the belief in many gods. In polytheistic religions, there are usually a great number of gods who are each in charge of a specific part of our natural world. The god of thunder, the god of wind, the god of the ocean, the god of rain, the god of fire, and it goes on and on. These gods spend eternity competing with one another. For instance, the god of rain may lose to the god of the sun for a time and the ensuing result is drought. The god of pestilence (sickness) may win over the god of well-being and the ensuing result is a plague. And on and on it goes. In the end, humans don't stand a chance! Sure, once in a while some god will decide that he or she likes you for some reason and does something nice for you. On the whole, you are stuck in the middle of their petty, little turf wars, which leave you a victim of fate. If fate would have it that you happen to be at the wrong place at the wrong time and the god of some volcano next to the town you are visiting blows his top, you are done. Fate is not a kind master. These forms of religion are fraught with fear and anxiety.

Monotheism – A Religion of Service

Monotheism is different. There are only three major monotheistic religions in the world today. Two of them are born out of the original. When Abraham began to tell the world about the One God of Heaven all the way back in Genesis, he was living in a polytheistic culture. While everyone else was trying to appease this god or that one, Abraham was hearing from and doing his best to serve the One God of all things. In following that One God, Abraham established Judaism: The religion of the Jewish people. The primary scripture of that religion is what we know as the Old Testament. To us, the God of the Old Testament seems to be angry and vengeful. Then again, we are attempting to judge an ancient practice against our modern expectations. When we attempt to shift and see the God of the Old Testament from an ancient perspective, we start to find a lot of love, compassion, forgiveness, and patience in Him. We start to see the fledgling roots of a God who would love the world so much that He would give, while all other ancient gods are taking from mankind. God instead chooses to give back. These traits almost are entirely missing from the gods of the people groups around ancient Israel. But these traits are imprinted on the hearts of the followers of this God, His chosen people, Israel.

Islam also is born out of Abraham. Though there is an entirely different scripture with them, the Koran, they trace their roots to the same Abraham that we meet in Genesis. The difference here is their prophet, Mohammad, who was a spiritual leader, a political leader, and a military leader. He was at times a vicious and effective warrior, and at other times a compassionate and caring teacher. All of these things are true of him, and therefore all of these things are true of his followers. Again, the traits of the founder are imprinted on the hearts of the followers.

Christianity comes directly out of Judaism and is based in the life, teachings, sacrificial death, and resurrection of Jesus told and taught in the New Testament. Jesus was a Jewish Carpenter and Rabbi. As our Founder, our Redeemer, our Savior, and our God, Jesus' traits are imprinted on the hearts of His followers.

Now think about it for a minute. If you are a follower of a polytheistic religious structure and your entire existence is based in fickle hands of fate (just hope you get lucky), you live in fear. You really don't have any other choice.

If you are a follower of an Old Testament, law-based religious structure, like Judaism, then your entire existence is based on your ability to properly follow the law. You live in constant fear that you will mess up and get it wrong. You really don't have any other choice.

If you are a follower of Mohammad, then you are insistent that the political and military leaders around you enforce adherence to your religious beliefs through their laws and warriors. You may live in fear, but you certainly cause fear among all those around you who may not hold to your particular religious beliefs.

If you are a follower of Jesus, then you instinctively know that your God expects of you sacrifice, forgiveness, service, and, most importantly, love for others. Jesus' entire message to us is all about love: *" 'Love the Lord your God with all your heart and with all your soul and with all your mind.' This is the first and greatest commandment. And the second is like it: 'Love your neighbor as yourself.' All the Law and the Prophets hang on these two commandments"* (Matthew 22:37-40).

If this is the message, then we do not need to live in fear. We do not need to cause anyone around us who disagrees with us to live in fear. Jesus has come to love every one of us. He has come to forgive us, redeem us, pay the price for us, and set us free from the fear that was once so dominant in our thinking and beliefs. When we live out this message, the people around us do not have anything to fear. We are not here to dominate them. We are not here to destroy them. We are not here to force them to believe in our God. We are here to love them until they see that our God is worth believing. Now we can understand what the Apostle is actually trying to say to us when he says this: *"This is how love is made complete among us so that we will have confidence* [not fear] *on the day of judgment: In this world we are like Jesus. There is no fear in love. But perfect love drives out fear, because fear has to do with punishment.* [Jesus has to do with forgiveness.] *The one who fears is not made perfect in love."*

Like Jesus ... we love.

Like Jesus ... we forgive.

Like Jesus ... we sacrifice.

Like Jesus ... we serve.

Like Jesus ... we set free.

Like Jesus ... we live.

By living like Jesus, we drive out fear.

Day 7

"We love because he first loved us. Whoever claims to love God yet hates a brother or sister is a liar. For whoever does not love their brother and sister, whom they have seen, cannot love God, whom they have not seen. And he has given us this command: Anyone who loves God must also love their brother and sister." (1 John 4:19-21)

Show Love to See God

All of this talk about love can often leave us wondering what has happened to the Church?

God so loved us that He gave to us.

Jesus so loved us that He died for us.

The Holy Spirit so loved us that He dwells in us.

We seem to have trouble being nice to each other much less nice to the world around us that does not know our God. Why? The Apostle is pretty blunt about this: *"Whoever claims to love God yet hates a brother or sister is a liar."* The word for *"brother"* is the Greek word *adelphos* (Blue Letter Bible). While this word can mean your brother or sister from the same parents, it also can mean brothers or sisters of like faith. So what the Apostle John is saying here is that we must love our fellow believers, brothers and sisters in Christ. If we don't love them but say we love God, then we're lying. Honestly, in today's church, we are in grave danger of being liars. We desperately need to relearn the art of seeing and thereby showing the love of God.

See God's Love in His Creation

"We love because he first loved us."

God loved us first. What a wonderful truth! When we read the words, *"he first loved us,"* we naturally think of the sacrifice that Jesus made for us on the cross. That is certainly the central story in all of human history. Jesus' sacrifice for us shows the depth of the Father's love for us and the lengths to which Jesus was willing to go in order to set us free and redeem us from sin.

But the story of God's love began long before the arrival of Jesus in Bethlehem.

Let's go back ... way back. At some point before the beginning of what we know as time, the Father, the Son, and the Holy Spirit considered the creation of all mankind. It was clear to them, as everything is clear to them, that mankind would fail. Sin would enter the creation through the rebellion of humans, specifically Adam and Eve. They realized that the sin of mankind would require a price. That price would be the death and resurrection of Jesus. He would be required to come here, become part of the creation, live, teach, suffer, and ultimately die. They further realized that mankind would not make it on our own. So the Holy Spirit would have to do the never-ending work of walking alongside and living in and with all humans. All of the costs, trials, failures, bloodshed, and sorrow of mankind was clearly seen by all three Persons of the Trinity. A choice had to be made. One would think that after looking at all of the horrors of human history, God would simply choose not to create this old world.

But He did create us. Why?

The answer is simple. Not only did God see the sorrow and pain, but He saw the goodness and love. For every act of evil, God saw thousands of moms kissing their babies as they comforted them to sleep. For every drop of blood spilled, God saw thousands of acts of kindness. For every human that would curse Him, He saw some that would praise Him, worship Him, and serve Him. God saw what news reporters tend to miss. There is much more to love than to fear about humans and this world. There is more good than bad. More love than hatred. More God than Satan.

God saw all of that ... and loved us ... enough to pay the price of creating us!

And here we are!

See God's Love in His People
"Whoever claims to love God yet hates a brother or sister is a liar. For whoever does not love their brother and sister, whom they have seen, cannot love God, whom they have not seen. And he has given us this command: Anyone who loves God must also love their brother and sister."

For all of that good news, it is still not always easy to love. I have said it so many times, but let me say it again. It will be helpful here.

Love is not a feeling; it is a choice of the will.

We are commanded to love our fellow believers in Christ. It is more than just to tolerate them, put up with them, and be nice to them. We are called to love them, and that is not an easy task. Love is not our default position as we have already discussed. Not all of our brothers and sisters are really all that loveable! But God says to do it anyway. God says that we, like He did, must choose to love others, even when we don't feel like it.

God could not command us to love if it was just a feeling. How is God going to command us to have a feeling? That's just not fair. Here is where the understanding breaks down these days. Most people do view love primarily as a feeling. Then when they read something like this where God commands us to love, they feel that God is commanding something unfairly. They protest and say: "I can't make myself feel something!" But God isn't commanding a feeling. He is commanding a choice. Remember, the word for love when it comes to God is *agape*, unconditional love. That is what we are to choose. At any given moment, in any given relationship, we are faced with a choice. Am I going to choose to love this person or am I going to choose to give into my feelings? Sometimes the struggle is not so great. Sometimes we actually feel like loving certain people. Other times, the struggle is real and we face people who are rude, difficult, not like us in any way, not understanding, and not kind. In a moment like that, we can easily get on board with tolerance. But how do we love? How do you even do that?

You choose.

You choose against anger.

You choose against resentment.

You choose against hurt.

You choose against bias.

You choose against arrogance.

You choose against all of that and ... in the power of the Holy Spirit ...

You choose love.

Since you love God, you choose to love your brothers and sisters.

And that is what God calls a Church!

WEEK

5

Day 1

"Everyone who believes that Jesus is the Christ is born of God, and everyone who loves the father loves his child as well. This is how we know that we love the children of God: by loving God and carrying out his commands. In fact, this is love for God: to keep his commands. And his commands are not burdensome, for everyone born of God overcomes the world. This is the victory that has overcome the world, even our faith. Who is it that overcomes the world? Only the one who believes that Jesus is the Son of God." (1 John 5:1-5)

A New Life
"Everyone who believes that Jesus is the Christ is born of God."

Are you born again? That question has taken a place in our modern American culture that is somewhere between a joke and a threat. Our society doesn't understand what that question means. It is one of those phrases that as a pastor I have to explain every time I use it. Jesus first defines the experience when he encounters a Pharisee named Nicodemus. This man is a teacher of the law and by all rights should view Jesus as an enemy. He realizes this and decides to come to Jesus at night, likely in secret, and make a startling confession: *"Rabbi, we know that you are a teacher who has come from God. For no one could perform the signs you are doing if God were not with him"* (John 3:2). This Pharisee knows Jesus is the real deal. He indicates that there are others like him who would denounce Jesus in daylight but confess they believe Him under cover of darkness. Jesus challenges him: *"Very truly I you, no one can see the kingdom of God unless they are born again"* (John 3:3). What? Then Nicodemus' question is really quite logical: *"How can someone be born when they are old?"* (John 3:4). All he is seeing is the physical. Physical miracles. Physical healings. Physical Jesus. Physical birth.

But that is where he has it all wrong.

Jesus speaks again, *"Very truly I tell you, no one can enter the kingdom of God unless they are born of water and the Spirit. Flesh gives birth to flesh, but the Spirit gives birth to spirit"* (John 3:5-6). Nicodemus is only seeing the surface of what Jesus is doing, but Jesus wants him to see deeper. Jesus wants him to understand that this new life that is being offered to so many will require a spiritual change. People will no longer depend on the physical following of laws for salvation. Instead, the day is coming when the Holy Spirit of God will birth within every believer a new life through the blood of Jesus and sustained by the power of the Holy Spirit.

A New Love
"And everyone who loves the father loves his child as well."

Once we have been born again, everything changes! What we once found impossible in our own strength, we now can accomplish through the forgiveness of Christ and the presence of the Holy Spirit. Listen to how the Apostle Paul describes it here: *"Therefore, if anyone is in Christ, the new creation has come: The old has gone, the new is here!"* (2 Corinthians 5:17). Before being born again, loving the children of God was, at best, difficult and, at worst, impossible. We struggled just to love ourselves much less those difficult folks down at the church! Now that we have been born again, we have a love for the Father God in Heaven, and somehow that has released in us the ability to love His people. Now don't get me wrong. It still is sometimes difficult and it is a choice we have to make every day. Through the cleansing power of the blood of Christ and the sanctifying power of the Holy Spirit, what once was impossible is now becoming natural!

A New Command
"This is how we know that we love the children of God: by loving God and carrying out his commands. In fact, this is love for God: to keep his commands. And his commands are not burdensome."

Our new birth also empowers us to see, understand, and live out the word of God. We can *"keep his commands"* because we have come to love God and His children. We *"keep his commands"* and *"love the children of God"* because it's not what we have to do but what we desire. It is an entirely new way of looking at our lives. Before, someone might ask: "OK fine. It's a drag, but what do I have to do to follow Jesus? I mean I don't want to go to hell and I don't want to tick God off, so tell me the bottom line. What is the minimum requirement to be a child of God?" With that defeated attitude, following God's commands is nothing more than a burdensome task. But now that I follow Him out of love instead of following Him out of mere necessity, His commands are not burdensome. In fact, I can follow God with joy because I follow Him out of love for Him and a knowledge that everything He calls me to do is actually going to make me better!

A New Victory

"For everyone born of God overcomes the world. This is the victory that has overcome the world, even our faith. Who is it that overcomes the world? Only the one who believes that Jesus is the Son of God."

When I follow God out of love and know He is making me a better, more godly person every day, I can't lose! Finally, I can see the world and its philosophies for what they really are. The things that the world values are worthless compared to Christ! The things that the world calls fun are painful and devastating compared to Christ! I can finally see that following Him makes me more, and following the world makes me less. In my new life, born again and made new, I can follow His commands with joy and overcome the world with confidence!

Day 2

"This is the one who came by water and blood—Jesus Christ. He did not come by water only, but by water and blood. And it is the Spirit who testifies, because the Spirit is the truth. For there are three that testify: the Spirit, the water and the blood; and the three are in agreement." (1 John 5:6-8)

As we take on these three verses, you should know that there are multiple takes on exactly what the Apostle is saying here. Let me tell you what I see.

There are three elements involved in the Apostle's description and all three are very important to the life of the believer. I believe that each element plays an indispensable role in our salvation and sanctification. I believe that leaving out any of these three things leaves the believer, at the very least, wandering and, at the very worst, lost.

The Testimony of the Water

The water mentioned here is the water of baptism. You may remember that we discussed the story of Jesus speaking to Nicodemus, the Pharisee, about being born again. Listen again to one sentence in Jesus' discussion with old Nic: *"Very truly I tell you, no one can enter the kingdom of God unless they are born of water and the Spirit"* (John 3:5). Here it is clear that Jesus is speaking of baptism, which is something He has subjected Himself to under the ministry of John the Baptist. In doing this, Jesus makes the ritual of baptism a sacrament of the Church that will be established in His Name. Christians get baptized.

I am not suggesting, as someone is likely thinking right now, that baptism is required for salvation. I believe strongly that every Christian should be baptized, but I don't see any support in scripture for the argument that the act of baptism can save anyone. Again, the Apostle Paul in Ephesians said, *"For it is by grace you have been saved, through faith—and this is not from yourselves, it is the gift of God—not by works, so that no one can boast"* (Ephesians 2:8). We are saved by grace through faith. No act of the church is necessary, just faith in Christ Jesus.

That doesn't mean the Church is unnecessary and baptism unimportant. In fact, I believe what the Apostle John is telling us here is that the sacramental work of the Church is of tremendous importance. As the Apostle enumerates the evidence to a truly changed life, he starts with the witness of the Church. That is the meaning of baptism. It is an individual coming in front of a given local church and declaring by baptism that they have accepted Christ and found a new life in Him. This is the public coming-out of a new believer, and John says that this witness is one of three that establishes the reality of our conversion!

The Testimony of the Blood

In the Gospel of John, we don't get *"blood"* as one of the witnesses, only *"water and the Spirit."* Keep in mind that in the Gospel of John, Jesus is speaking pre-crucifixion, so the blood has not yet been shed. Then here in the Epistle of John, we are post-crucifixion and post-resurrection. The Apostle can now see the full picture of what Jesus was laying the groundwork for in his conversation with Nicodemus. Now we understand that salvation is not simply an act of the Church. Baptism, for all of its importance and symbolism, is worthless without the blood of Jesus being shed for the forgiveness of our sins. In Hebrews, the writer clearly reminds us that, *"the law requires that nearly everything be cleansed with blood, and without the shedding of blood there is no forgiveness"* (Hebrews 9:22). Jesus sacrificed Himself for our sins. *"The death he died, he died to sin once for all"* (Romans 6:10). The truth of this is given further clarity in Romans, chapter 5:

> *Nor can the gift of God be compared with the result of one man's sin* [Adam]: *The judgment followed one sin and brought condemnation, but the gift followed many trespasses and brought justification. For if, by the trespass of the one man, death reigned through that one man, how much more will those who receive God's abundant provision of grace and of the gift of righteousness reign in life through the one man, Jesus Christ! (Romans 5:16-17)*

It is the blood of Jesus that brings salvation.

We now have the witness of the Church through the water of baptism that we are saved, and the witness of Christ through the blood of His sacrifice that we are saved. There is only one thing that remains.

The Testimony of the Spirit

Finally, there is the testimony of the Holy Spirit of God. It is the Spirit of God that draws us to the blood of Christ in the first place. The Holy Spirit speaks into our hearts and lets us know that we are missing something. He whispers into our very souls that we are in need of more than just a better day, some better breaks, or turning over a new leaf. The Spirit reminds us that we are lost and in need of forgiveness. Even when we act like we don't need to be forgiven of anything, the Holy Spirit is there reminding us, pushing us, nudging us, and drawing us. When we finally come over to God's side through Jesus' sacrifice, we discover that it is the Holy Spirit that gives us the power to be changed. The constant work of the Holy Spirit in our lives is what makes us truly different and new. That process of change boldly declares as a witness to the world that we have been redeemed.

Perhaps more importantly, the Holy Spirit whispers into our hearts and souls that we are still God's children during the dark nights of difficulty that we will inevitably face in this Christian walk. The darkness cannot steal that from us. Nothing can take us from the hand of a God who has paid the ultimate price for us and is willing to live in us in order to keep us close to Him.

So the witnesses cry out.

The Water – Through the sacraments and fellowship of the body of believers, the Church, we are declared new!

The Blood – Through the sacrifice and love of our Savior, Jesus Christ, we are declared new!

The Spirit – Through the indwelling presence and life-changing power of the Holy Spirit, we are declared new!

Day 3

"We accept human testimony, but God's testimony is greater because it is the testimony of God, which he has given about his Son. Whoever believes in the Son of God accepts this testimony. Whoever does not believe God has made him out to be a liar, because they have not believed the testimony God has given about his Son. And this is the testimony: God has given us eternal life, and this life is in his Son. Whoever has the Son has life; whoever does not have the Son of God does not have life." (1 John 5:9-12)

Everyone has an opinion, but not everyone has a clue. You would think that people without a clue would withhold their opinions, but that just isn't the case these days. Our culture is becoming increasingly insistent on constant commentary on every imaginable topic. Honestly, we have dedicated cable channels to all kinds of things. These channels talk about one subject 24 hours a day and 7 days a week. I have to be honest; I am not certain that all of those topics have enough content to fill those days and hours. For instance, there is a golf channel, fishing channel, history channel, and a few different food channels. Each of these, pontificate on and on about their particular area of focus. Really, how many times can a person learn how to fry a chicken? How many golf interviews can any person really watch? How many fishing trips can you try and understand?

Now since I am already offending all cooks, golfers, and fishermen, let me just go ahead and offend everyone else. We all have fallen prey to this idea that our opinion is somehow important and should always be expressed. I am afraid that just isn't entirely true. While it is fine in a nation that values freedom of speech to talk constantly, there isn't really value in it especially when you don't have the information necessary to say something true or helpful. In that cultural setting, people say all kinds of things about each other. They consistently "give testimony" to what they think is true of a person without ever really knowing if it is true or not. When there are gaps in their understanding, they just make stuff up that sounds like it fits.

While these rumor mills are aggravating, they need not concern us too much. The Apostle John directly comes at this issue and clearly points out that it is only the testimony of God that matters. God's testimony is always true and always right. The Spirit of God living in us is the one who knows what is actually true about us. One commentator talking about this particular verse puts it this way:

> In its daily experience, the soul finds ever fresh proof that the declaration, 'This is my beloved Son,' is true. But even without this internal corroboration, the external evidence suffices, and he who rejects it makes God a liar; for it is God who presents the evidence, and presents it as sufficient and true. (Spence and Exell 1950, p. 141)

Regardless of what people think, when we receive Jesus as our Savior and God declares us to be His children, we ARE children of the King. The world can say what it will, but the testimony of God is all that matters.

Furthermore, when the world around us attempts to deny the truth within us, they are actually not insulting us at all. They are insulting God. Look at it this way. I am not the one who declared myself a child of God; God did. I am not the one who declared sins forgiven; God did. I am not the one who declared I have eternal life; God did. When someone questions my position in Christ, they are not so much calling me a liar; they are calling God a liar. He is my only Judge and His opinion is the only one that ultimately matters.

So let the world yammer on! Let them spout their opinions all day, every day. In the end, my job is to truly live out the grace of God that has been placed in me, and in doing so establish the ultimate truth. In the Epistle of John: *"And this is the testimony: God has given us eternal life, and this life is in his Son. Whoever has the Son has life; whoever does not have the Son of God does not have life."* In the Gospel of John: *"So if the Son sets you free, you will be free indeed"* (John 8:36).

Day 4

"I write these things to you who believe in the name of the Son of God so that you may know that you have eternal life. This is the confidence we have in approaching God: that if we ask anything according to his will, he hears us. And if we know that he hears us—whatever we ask—we know that we have what we asked of him." (1 John 5:13-15)

Here the Apostle begins to wrap up his letter. As he moves toward a conclusion, he wants to make sure that we confidently know what our life in Christ has done for us. His call for us has taken on many facets. These include that we *"walk in the light, as he is in the light"* (1 John 1:7); we *"not sin"* (1 John 2:1); we know that *"we should be called children of God!"* (1 John 3:1); we *"love one another as he* [Christ] *commanded us"* (1 John 3:23); we *"not love the world or anything in the world"* (1 John 2:15); we know that *"many antichrists have come"* (1 John 2:18); and we *"not believe every spirit, but test the spirits to see whether they are from God"* (1 John 4:1). All of this applied appropriately changes us. These things make us better, stronger, kinder, more loving, and more spiritually grounded. They make us more like Christ. In doing so, they give us a renewed, informed, and empowered confidence in our lives and in our relationship with God.

Confidently Saved

"I write these things to you who believe in the name of the Son of God so that you may know that you have eternal life."

Our salvation is no insecure thing, especially when we are applying all of the truths given to us by the Apostle John in this letter. Look, God has given His all in order to restore a relationship with mankind. He is not, after paying that price, looking to break that relationship again. As I was growing up, our family always attended holiness churches. Back in the day, these churches were all about getting someone to come down to the altar and confess sin and find forgiveness. Now I am not saying that there is anything wrong with that; people need to come to Christ confessing sin and finding forgiveness. However, all too often, the goal was getting people to the altar. If the preacher needed to convince you that you were not as secure as you thought you were in order to get you to that altar, he would do it! The masters at this were the traveling evangelists. They would preach young believers right into hell in order to get them to the altar and save them again! (I think I "got saved" dozens of times!) It was really a spiritual roller coaster.

Now it was probably good for me to be wary about my salvation. My desires and tendencies as a young man were not often pure and godly. Nonetheless, it was biblically unnecessary. The God who paid the high cost of our salvation is not sitting in Heaven with a lightning bolt looking for a chance to knock us off! With that said, we should be careful how we live and constantly search our hearts and lives for sin that needs to be confessed and forgiven ... but that is different than living in insecurity. So be confident in your salvation through Christ Jesus, and respect that salvation enough to live rightly inside of it!

Confidently Praying

"This is the confidence we have in approaching God: that if we ask anything according to his will, he hears us."

Since we have this relationship with God through Christ and led by the Holy Spirit, we can pray differently. In most other religious belief systems, there is always a practice of approaching prayer with at least some level of fear. Get in the right position. Pray during the right hour. Face the right direction. Say the right words. It can become rather stressful. With Christianity, there is no such stress. We are to have confidence when approaching God. The writer of Hebrews gives even greater clarity to this when he writes: *"Let us then approach God's throne of grace with confidence, so that we may receive mercy and find grace to help us in our time of need"* (Hebrews 4:16). In both cases, the writers use a word that is translated to *"confidence."* The Greek word here is *parresia*, which is often translated as "boldness" (Blue Letter Bible). So we can approach God with boldness because of the fact that we are now *"children of God."* What an amazing truth!

This is not to be taken as permission to approach God with anything less than respect. He is, after all, still God. When we practice the things that the Apostle has called us to here in his letter, not only do our actions change but also our attitudes toward God change. They become sanctified, or set apart for sacred use, and Christ-centered instead of self-centered. McGee (1983) puts it this way: "If we are in fellowship with Him, if we are not regarding sin in our lives, and if there are no other hindrances to prayer in our lives, we are not going to pray selfishly" (p. 819). So our confidence is based not only in our adoption as children of God, but also in our transformation into people of God. McGee goes a bit further in his description of how our prayer life should function: "We are not to come to Him with mistrust or in a begging attitude, but we are to come with boldness to ask that God's will be done" (p. 819).

Confidently Believing

"And if we know that he hears us—whatever we ask—we know that we have what we asked of him."

People will often ask me, "Pastor how can I have a powerful prayer life?" The answer is not complex. However, the answer is also not so easy. If you want to have a powerful prayer life, then you must do everything possible to assure that you are praying in accordance with the will of God. Simply put, God's will is going to happen. Everything that is God's will is going to happen. In other words, our small opinions, desires, and preferences are not going to change the ultimate and perfect will of God. If we can learn to surrender to the Holy Spirit and know the heart of God in such a way as to be praying in His will, then our prayers will always come to pass. Of course, this is not always possible. Honestly, sometimes we don't want what God wants even when we should. It is in these moments that it may seem our prayers go unanswered.

But they don't.

God always answers prayers.

I have heard many pastors say that God answers prayers in one of three ways:

1. Yes (This is the answer we always want!)

2. No (OK, this one is really tough!)

3. Wait (This may be the most difficult of all!)

When God calls us to wait, it can seem that He is not listening to us. It can seem that our prayers have gone unanswered, but that is just simply not the case. God always hears the prayers of His children, and He always answers those prayers. The commentary writer put it this way: "It may be years before we perceive that our prayers have been answered: perhaps in this world we may never be able to see this; but we *know* that God *has* answered them" (Spence and Exell 1950, p. 141). So we can pray with great confidence knowing that God hears us and will answer us, even when it seems that He has chosen not to answer. The problem is not in His willingness to answer. The problem is in our ability to understand and comprehend the actions of the Almighty. We must stand in confidence. Confidence not in our prayer life or our wisdom, but confidence in our Father who clearly said, *"Never will I leave you; never will I forsake you"* (Hebrews 13:5).

Day 5

"If you see any brother or sister commit a sin that does not lead to death, you should pray and God will give them life. I refer to those whose sin does not lead to death. There is a sin that leads to death. I am not saying that you should pray about that. All wrongdoing is sin, and there is sin that does not lead to death." (1 John 5:16-17)

These are difficult verses. We are immediately struck by the idea that *"there is a sin that leads to death."* We want to know what that means. I will give you two takes on the meaning of this phrase, and then we will talk about what the verses are trying to say to us.

Sin that Leads to Death

There are many different opinions on this and the meaning behind it. Let me give one that I don't agree with and then lay out what I think is the most plausible understanding. First of all, let's set aside any thought of the unpardonable sin that is spelled out for us by Jesus in Matthew 12:30-32, Mark 3:28-30, and Luke 12:8-10. What the Apostle is referring to here is not the same thing that Jesus is talking about in those verses. While the trespasses may have some commonality, these are two different issues.

Sin that Leads to Physical Death

Some reject the idea that this *"sin that leads to death"* could possibly be a spiritual death. These folks are generally from the "once saved, always saved" crowd. Their doctrine of eternal security would not allow for the idea that a believer could possibly commit a sin that would lead to spiritual death. While I normally agree with J. Vernon McGee, this is a point on which we differ. So to be fair to this doctrine that I do not hold, let me give you a sample of his take on this verse:

> 'Death' refers here to *physical* death. It has no reference at all to spiritual death because the child of God has eternal life. John is saying that believers can commit a sin for which their heavenly Father will call them home; that is, He will remove them from this life physically, perhaps because they are disgracing Him. (McGee 1983, p. 819)

So in McGee's doctrine on this matter, the Father God in Heaven sort of becomes a divine executioner who performs honor killings.

I have to say that while a lot of people take this position, I just don't get it. There is no reason that I can see in the language that this word rendered *"death"* would be restricted to physical death. The Greek word used here is *thanatos*, which works much like our word for the same thing, death (Blue Letter Bible). It would be entirely appropriate to use the word *"death"* to describe the end of spiritual life or the end of physical life. It is not the language that prevents McGee and others from reading this as spiritual death; instead, it is the doctrine that prevents it.

Sin that Leads to Spiritual Death

The second viewpoint would be that this *"sin that leads to death"* could be referring to a physical OR spiritual death. In this instance, we would imagine a believer who has chosen to walk away from his or her faith in Christ, and in doing so has forfeited the grace that comes from faith. Some might argue that such a thing is not possible, but consider this verse out of Hebrews:

> *It is impossible for those who have once been enlightened, who have tasted the heavenly gift, who have shared in the Holy Spirit, who have tasted the goodness of the word of God and the powers of the coming age and who have fallen away, to be brought back to repentance. To their loss they are crucifying the Son of God all over again and subjecting him to public disgrace. (Hebrews 6:4-6)*

That sounds to me like a pretty clear description of what the Apostle John would call *"a sin that leads to death."* If someone has gone that far away from their faith, then your prayers are of little help. The writer in the Pulpit Commentary gives the explanation that is most suitable to me:

> If God's will does not override man's will, neither can a fellow-man's prayer. When a human will has been firmly and persistently set in opposition to the Divine will, our intercession will be of no avail. And this seems to be the meaning of 'sin unto death;'

[sin that leads to death] wilful and obstinate rejection of God's grace and persistence in unrepented sin. (Spence and Exell 1950, p. 142)

Now, take a moment and breathe. Someone is reading this and wondering if somehow they have committed this *"sin that leads to death"* and therefore condemned themselves unintentionally. Listen carefully to what I am about to boldly state.

THIS CANNOT OCCUR UNINTENTIONALLY. IF YOU ARE WORRIED ABOUT IT, YOU HAVEN'T DONE IT!!!

In every way of looking at this, a sin, rejecting God at this level, is intentional, brutal, difficult, and long term. Once a person has gone this far away, the Holy Spirit will leave them alone and let them live in their own delusion for the remainder of their days here on earth. God will not force anyone into salvation nor will He trap anyone in a salvation they no longer wish to maintain. Free will just doesn't work that way.

Pray for people who are caught in sin.

Let's go back.

Having dealt with the shocking part of this verse, let's remember what it is actually saying: *"If you see any brother or sister commit a sin that does not lead to death, you should pray and God will give them life."* You know, we need to hear this. We are much better at condemning people for their sins than we are at praying that God would deliver them from their sins. The command is for prayer. By the way, if you are actually walking in the light of God and living in the love of God, how could you not pray for a fellow sister or brother who is caught up in sin? This should be our natural response. The Apostle reminds us of what we should already know ... and what we should already be doing.

Day 6

"We know that anyone born of God does not continue to sin; the One who was born of God keeps them safe, and the evil one cannot harm them. We know that we are children of God, and that the whole world is under the control of the evil one. We know also that the Son of God has come and has given us understanding, so that we may know him who is true. And we are in him who is true by being in his Son Jesus Christ. He is the true God and eternal life." (1 John 5:18-20)

Sanctification

"We know that anyone born of God does not continue to sin."

Here again we get the call of the Apostle John to a life that is free of sin. As he draws his letter to a close, he wants to revisit the main ideas of his letter for his *"dear children"* who will be reading the letter. He is imploring them to avoid sinful behavior. Avoid willful transgression of God's known laws. Avoid doing wrong. You know, over time we come to know more and more about God's laws and God's expectations of us. The more we know, the more we are responsible to follow. God is intentional about that. The Holy Spirit consistently reveals to us precisely the things He wants us to avoid, stop doing, or get away from. There is a consistent presence of God's Spirit that is constantly leading.

I often am amazed as I deliver sermons at what people hear from what I know I just said. Afterwards, a person will come up to me and declare that I spoke "right to them" on a particular issue. While I can see how that could be taken from my words, it was not what I was attempting to communicate. Now you might think that is an indication that I need to improve my communication skills, and maybe I do, but I think there is something else going on here. The Holy Spirit miraculously communicates through preachers' mouths every day. More importantly, the Holy Spirit miraculously opens listeners' ears and hearts every day! In the powerful presence of the Holy Spirit, people hear what God wants them to hear, and it changes them if they let it!

Safety
"The One who was born of God keeps them safe, and the evil one cannot harm them."

Here is another concern I get regularly. Fear. Read these words again, *"the One who was born of God keeps them safe, and the evil one cannot harm them."*

The evil one CANNOT harm them!

Find peace in those words. Find safety in those words. Find hope in those words. Find the ability to sleep in those words. When I was a child, I often would find myself terrified in the dark. At the time, I'm not sure why I was so afraid, but I was. In my own mind, I decided I needed to figure this thing out. There was a Bible verse that helped me from 1 John. Let me give it to you in the King James Version because that is how I first heard and memorized the verse:

"Ye are of God, little children, and have overcome them: because greater is he that is in you, than he that is in the world" (1 John 4:4). I would love to tell you that I learned this verse in a great sermon or wonderful Sunday school lesson, but I didn't. Our children's choir sang a song and that verse was the central theme of the song, and I remembered it. I would lay in my bed in the dark alone and afraid, but I would imagine my God who was in me guarding and protecting me. I found peace in that, and then I could sleep. As an adult, those terrifying nights are uncommon. However, once in a while for whatever reason, one will come and I still sing that little song in my head and visualize that greater God protecting me, His little child.

Security

"We know that we are children of God, and that the whole world is under the control of the evil one. We know also that the Son of God has come and has given us understanding, so that we may know him who is true. And we are in him who is true by being in his Son Jesus Christ. He is the true God and eternal life."

A Secure Home

"We know that we are children of God."

There are maybe only a few bits of knowledge more important than that one. As God's children, we are at home in His presence. As His children, we are secure in our relationship with Him. He has adopted us through the redeeming work of His Son, Jesus. *"But when the set time had fully come, God sent his Son, born of a woman, born under the law, to redeem those under the law, that we might receive adoption to sonship. Because you are his sons, God sent the Spirit of his Son into our hearts, the Spirit who calls out, 'Abba, Father'"* (Galatians 4:4-6).

A Secure Understanding

God has given us understanding. One of the goals of my ministry is to help people realize that they can understand the word of God, the Bible. It is not that pastors, preachers, and theologians are unnecessary. Each plays a role in the healthy progress of the Church, the body of Christ. However, understanding is given to every child of God. Part of the security we find in Him is the fact that He will help us understand what He is saying to us through His word. It concerns me when people don't look into the word for themselves. I don't want to be the only source of God's word in your life! I am not nearly enough! You look at it, and by the power of God you can understand.

A Secure Savior

"And we are in him who is true by being in his Son Jesus Christ. He is the true God and eternal life."

There is an old song written by Andrea Crouch that often rings in the back of my mind. The lyrics go something like this:

> Jesus is the answer, for the world today.
> Above Him there's no other, Jesus is the way.

He is truly our hope. There is no other above Him. Jesus is the way! Oh, if we could remember that on difficult days. Oh, if we could remember that on dark days. Oh, if we could remember that on every day! Jesus is the answer!

Day 7

"Dear children, keep yourselves from idols." (1 John 5:21)

As the Apostle John wraps up his first letter, he ends on this note, *"keep yourselves from idols."* It may seem like a warning that is misplaced with us these days. We don't exactly have idols hanging around in our town squares and lurking inside of our homes. Idolatry, as it was practiced in the first century, is not really part of our culture.

Or is it?

An idol is really nothing more than the form of a false god. So we need to avoid false gods in our lives, but that brings up the question: What is a god? For that, let me lay some groundwork. The Greek word here is *Theos*, which is translated as a deity or a supreme divinity. The definition can even extend to a magistrate or ruler (Blue Letter Bible). In short, a god is anything that has been given control over your life. It is anything that has the authority to direct your life or your choices. A god can be anything that becomes the final authority in your life. While many things may affect a choice you make, there is one overriding authority, one overarching power, and one issue that is more important than any other.

That one thing is your god.

All too often, that one thing is not the God of the Bible.

If we are honest with ourselves, we have to admit that many things are given precedence over the God of the Bible and the word of God in our lives. There are moments in every life where some priority, pressure, person, or desire is allowed to outweigh or overrule what we know to be biblical truth or righteous living. In that moment, that thing becomes our god. It is what I like to call a "small g" god. The title for this god is not capitalized because there is no real authority or power in this god, and it is just sin. It is sin because it is a willful rejection of God's law ("big G") in order to follow the call or allure of some desire or person that we have allowed to become a god ("small g") in our lives. This is clearly a willful transgression of a known law. It is clearly sin, and we need to avoid it.

Consider it this way. There is a throne in your heart, and someone or something occupies that throne. The person or thing that is on that throne is what controls you. You bow to it because you make all of your choices based on what feeds it, grows it, or serves it. You think about it constantly because it dominates your heart and therefore dominates your thoughts. You will reject anything or anyone who comes against it, even if you don't necessarily want to, because it is controlling you.

And that is the issue ... what is controlling you?

You might say: "But Pastor Mike, I am a free person and I can do what I want!" Yes, that is true. The issue is not about what you do but what controls you. The Apostle Paul spoke to this in 1 Corinthians: *" 'I have the right to do anything,' you say—but not everything is beneficial. 'I have the right to do anything'—but I will not be mastered by anything"* (1 Corinthians 6:12). The Apostle Paul was obviously *"mastered"* by the God of Heaven and by Jesus the Christ, but nothing else was going to be allowed on that throne. He was far more worried about what controlled his choices than he was about the specific choices themselves. The reason is obvious. I will serve what I place on the throne of my life. If the throne of my life is inhabited by an idol, a false god, then I will serve that false god. It is impossible to serve two gods at once! Therefore, if I am serving a false god, I am ignoring the true God.

So let me end with the same ending that the Apostle John used in his letter. Let me remind you that he writes to *"dear children."* This means people he truly loves and desires to protect from *"antichrists"* and *"false prophets,"* people he has warned to *"test the spirits,"* and people he desires to see *"walk in the light"* and learn to know and serve the God who is love. And so, as he wraps all of that up and as I close this section with you ... as the Holy Spirit seeks to guide you ... hear the warning because it is for you.

"Dear children, keep yourselves from idols."

WEEK

6

Day 1

II John

"The elder, To the lady chosen by God and to her children, whom I love in the truth—and not I only, but also all who know the truth—because of the truth, which lives in us and will be with us forever: Grace, mercy and peace from God the Father and from Jesus Christ, the Father's Son, will be with us in truth and love. It has given me great joy to find some of your children walking in the truth, just as the Father commanded us. And now, dear lady, I am not writing you a new command but one we have had from the beginning. I ask that we love one another. And this is love: that we walk in obedience to his commands. As you have heard from the beginning, his command is that you walk in love." (2 John 1:1-6)

As we read this short letter, we immediately recognize that the Apostle is writing *"to the lady ... and to her children."* He greets her in a very warm fashion recognizing that she is well thought-of and well-loved throughout the churches in the area. He then gives what is almost a universal greeting in the letters written by the Apostles throughout the New Testament: *"Grace, mercy and peace from God the Father and from Jesus Christ, the Father's Son, will be with us in truth and love."* I never miss a chance to point out the order of these words. It never changes. It always starts with grace and ends with peace. The peace of the Christian life is found solely in the grace extended by Christ, and you just can't get to peace until you go through grace!

As to the effectiveness of her ministry, the Apostle is impressed: *"It has given me great joy to find some of your children walking in the truth, just as the Father commanded us."* She has obviously found a way to teach the good news of Jesus to the people in her care in such a way that their faith remains strong and intact, even in the face of the confusion and persecution the first-century church was facing. She has built a strong group of believers, and I assure you that is no simple task!

He then begins the true message of his letter. I am going to break this into three sections. We will look at one each day.

Remember Love

"And now, dear lady, I am not writing you a new command but one we have had from the beginning. I ask that we love one another. And this is love: that we walk in obedience to his commands. As you have heard from the beginning, his command is that you walk in love."

The Apostle now lays the groundwork for what he needs her to understand. This leader, who has effectively led her people into a strong and resilient faith, is called to remember that we are commanded to *"walk in love."* This command plays out in two very distinct and yet connected ways. The first way is that when we walk in love, we love one another. The second way is that when we walk in love, we love God. That will drive us toward two different outcomes.

Walking in love with our brothers and sisters in Christ will drive us to serve, show kindness, forgive, and trust one another. This is, in fact, the mark of the Church of Jesus Christ. Jesus set the standard when He said, *"By this everyone will know that you are my disciples, if you love one another"* (John 13:35). The Apostle reminds her of what he so forcefully expressed in his first letter: *"Dear friends, let us love one another, for love comes from God"* (1 John 4:7).

Walking in love toward God will drive us to *"walk in obedience to his commands."* Loving God demands that we obey God. The Apostle reinforces one of the key teachings from his first letter: *"This is love for God: to keep his commands"* (1 John 5:3). When our love drives us to obey God, our obedience to Him can be born out of joyfulness instead of compulsion.

All of this can and should be clearly understood through the words of Jesus: *" 'Love the Lord your God with all your heart and with all your soul and with all your mind and with all your strength.'... 'Love your neighbor as yourself.' There is no commandment greater than these"* (Mark 12:30-31). When we learn to love like that, the righteousness of our lives begins to become a normal outflow of our love for God and others. While this kind of love is not always natural in people's lives, it becomes more natural as we become more like Him. As we continue in Christ and in a loving relationship with His children, we learn how to more effectively *"walk in love."*

Day 2

"I say this because many deceivers, who do not acknowledge Jesus Christ as coming in the flesh, have gone out into the world. Any such person is the deceiver and the antichrist. Watch out that you do not lose what we have worked for, but that you may be rewarded fully." (2 John 1:7-8)

Defend Truth

Over the course of decades of ministry, a pastor can run into many situations where a church member or another local pastor falls into false teaching. I have certainly seen my share of these occurrences. Let me be clear here. I am a part of the Wesleyan Church. This means that I am a Protestant, Arminian, denominational, holiness, and largely evangelical pastor. Many of you have no idea what all these words mean, and you really don't need to know in order to live a full and effective Christian life. Let me suffice it to say that this aligns me with a certain segment of those who claim Christianity. These words define my theology and biblical understanding. However, they do not define the outside edges of Christianity nor do these words define the boundaries of those who can be saved and Heaven-bound. For instance, they create a circle that does not include Baptists, Pentecostals, Charismatics, Presbyterians, Lutherans, Catholics, Orthodox, and many other groups. I, of course, do not believe that all of these groups are unsaved and hell-bound. That would be ridiculous!

When we are defending truth, we must be careful not to fight against ourselves. There are three words that you need to understand in order to know who to defend against and who to walk beside.

Opinion – written in pencil so it can be easily changed.

Everyone has an opinion! Opinions have never been in short supply within any church. The problem is that some folks have attempted to turn their opinion into doctrine. Listen very carefully. There is no doctrine of music style, lighting controls, sanctuary carpet color, windows, building style, congregation size, Bible translation used (as long as it is true to the original languages), dress code (as long as it is modest), or many other things that people fight about within churches. These are areas of opinion. To attempt to make them a matter of doctrine diminishes the actual importance of doctrines. Doctrines matter, and opinions largely don't matter. Doctrines last, and opinions change. Everything cannot be doctrine. When we attempt to doctrine-ize our opinions, we just create unnecessary church fights.

Doctrine – written in pen so it can be remembered and kept.

Actual doctrines are things that should be defended. I do not agree with all Christian doctrines. The Baptists believe some things I don't. The Catholics believe a lot of things I don't. The Pentecostals believe some things I don't. All of them don't believe some things I do. None of this diminishes the overall truth of who Christ is, the saving power of His blood, the sustaining presence of the Holy Spirit, or the eternal truth of scripture. These doctrines are important and they define how we think and act. They should never be easily changed or dismissed. They should be defended within the family of God and outside the family of God. Doctrines matter, and they also divide. Our doctrines aren't supposed to unite us; dogma does that.

Dogma – written in blood and defended to the death.

Defending truth, in the end, means defending dogma. Dogma defines those aspects of Christianity that are universally accepted by all people of Christian faith, and Christianity cannot be claimed without those things. The Apostle gives us a clear statement of dogma here. He, in fact, gives us a simple way to weed out those who are teaching acceptable truth and those who are not.

It's all about Jesus.

The reality of Jesus as both a historical figure and as God incarnate (God in the flesh) is central and inseparable from any true Christian belief system. Jesus is the answer and must remain the answer. Think of it this way. At the center of every other religious system of thought, is a set of ideas, rules, or doctrines put together by a person that became central to that religion. Why? Simple answer: They were the one who penned the thoughts. Had they not done it, someone else eventually would have. Had Confucius not penned his ideas, then someone else would have eventually written something similar and instead of Confucianism, we would have Harold-ism or something of the sort. Had Mohammad not penned his thoughts on God and right living, then someone else would have eventually penned something similar. Islam is only dependent on Mohammad as the Prophet. Confucianism is only dependent on Confucius as the thinker. And on it could go.

Christianity isn't like that.

Christianity is centered on and completely dependent on the person of Jesus. Anyone who denies that Jesus was a real person cannot be a Christian. Anyone who denies that Jesus was God incarnate cannot be a Christian. *"Any such person is the deceiver and the antichrist."* Therefore, always avoid folks who want to diminish the person or the deity (God-ness) of Jesus. These people are not speaking Christian doctrines. While you are at it, avoid people who talk more about themselves than they do about Jesus. Jesus is the answer, not some televangelist who wants you to write a check or some overpowering pastor who wants you to follow him and no one else. When the Church becomes about a man, it is no longer about Jesus, and that is just not OK.

Finally, with those you agree with, stop fighting. Baptists, Pentecostals, Charismatics, Presbyterians,

Lutherans, Catholics, Orthodox, and many other groups are not Wesleyan in their doctrines, but they are Christian! They all claim the humanity and the Deity of Jesus. They all seek forgiveness of sin through the blood of Jesus. They all seek the sustaining power of the Holy Spirit in their daily lives.

So don't fight with them ... walk with them ... as we all follow Jesus!

Day 3

"Anyone who runs ahead and does not continue in the teaching of Christ does not have God; whoever continues in the teaching has both the Father and the Son. If anyone comes to you and does not bring this teaching, do not take them into your house or welcome them. Anyone who welcomes them shares in their wicked work. I have much to write to you, but I do not want to use paper and ink. Instead, I hope to visit you and talk with you face to face, so that our joy may be complete. The children of your sister, who is chosen by God, send their greetings." (2 John 1:9-13)

When I was a child, our family attended a non-denominational church for a few years. The pastor was a wonderful preacher and had a pretty good grasp on his doctrine and theology, but he was one of those overbearing, dominant types. Well, he and my dad had a falling out, so my mom and dad decided that we would move on to another church home. They never were ones to cause or take part in conflict. Two weeks after we left the church, the pastor preached this verse from the pulpit: *"Anyone who welcomes them shares in their wicked work,"* and he applied that verse to my family. That Sunday afternoon, I called my best friend. You should know that all my friends were in that church. Upon answering the phone, he said to me: "I can't talk to you anymore. You guys are sinners and if we have anything to do with you, then we will be sinners too." Then he hung up. Honestly, we didn't reconnect until 30 years later. Let me tell you, that was a tough theology lesson for a 12-year old kid! Needless to say, the pastor had terribly misused that verse.

That does not negate the importance of this verse. We must defend our homes and our families from non-Christian doctrines and beliefs. The setting here is really quite simple. There were no radios, televisions, phones, or Internet. This new church was being taught and informed of truth by a network of traveling pastors and teachers who were taught by the Apostles. The custom was that when one of these traveling teachers would come to town, some prominent and often wealthy family would take them in and take care of them while they were there teaching. It was an honor to do this, and it was the only way these traveling pastors could sustain themselves. In this case, the Apostle is writing to a prominent woman in some town who has been housing these traveling teachers, but she has recently housed some teachers who are not from the Apostles. These teachers were Gnostics. We already have discussed their errant beliefs. They do not accept that Jesus is God, and they teach that all material or physical things are evil. These beliefs are not compatible with Christianity. So the Apostle John is warning her about these *"antichrists."*

It is likely that he writes this short letter at about the same time he writes the much longer letter of 1 John. In his first letter he is addressing the entire body of believers. In this one, he is specifically addressing this one woman. We all should hear his warning to her. While kindness and hospitality should always be a mark of the Christian life, we also should be vigilant about defending truth within our homes. Our families and the homes we live in should not be exposed to wrong teaching and anti-Christian rhetoric. We just shouldn't allow that kind of thing in our house. In her effort to be kind, this woman has exposed her household to teaching that could be destructive to the Church in general as well as to her family. Such a risk should never be taken.

In her day, this practice was really pretty cut and dry. A guy comes to the door and wants to stay a while so he can teach at the local church. He doesn't believe in Jesus, so you say no. Simple. Nowadays, it isn't so simple. With the connectedness of our world through media and the Internet, we could easily be hosting ideas and teaching that is nowhere near truth! It can be happening without us even realizing what is going on. I believe that in today's hyper-connected world, the role of a parent is truly daunting. We simply must defend our homes and our families. Our children are being inundated with images and thoughts that are not consistent with biblical truth, and we are called narrow-minded, bigoted, or even abusive if we attempt to guard them from these influences.

Well, let me be clear.

Do not allow yourself to be bullied by the world!

Defend your family by taking control of the media in your home!

You may not be able to control what your children are exposed to by the school system they are in or by their friends. However, to the greatest degree possible, protect them. Yes, they will need to know about all of that stuff at some point so they can defend themselves when they are older. Until then, do all that you can to be the arbiter of that exposure. Talk them through why some websites are not OK. Talk them through why Jesus is the answer. Talk them through why some influences are good and others are bad. The world is out there telling them lies. You must do the work of telling them truth. If some false prophet comes to your door claiming that Jesus is not God, then you will know what to do.

"Anyone who runs ahead and does not continue in the teaching of Christ does not have God; whoever continues in the teaching has both the Father and the Son. If anyone comes to you and does not bring this teaching, do not take them into your house or welcome them."

Not my words ... the Apostle John said it!

Day 4

III John

"The elder, To my dear friend Gaius, whom I love in the truth. Dear friend, I pray that you may enjoy good health and that all may go well with you, even as your soul is getting along well. It gave me great joy when some believers came and testified about your faithfulness to the truth, telling how you continue to walk in it. I have no greater joy than to hear that my children are walking in the truth. Dear friend, you are faithful in what you are doing for the brothers and sisters, even though they are strangers to you. They have told the church about your love. Please send them on their way in a manner that honors God. It was for the sake of the Name that they went out, receiving no help from the pagans. We ought therefore to show hospitality to such people so that we may work together for the truth." (3 John 1:1-8)

As the Apostle John writes his third letter, He addresses it to an individual, similar to his previous letter. He writes to a man named Gaius. John seems to have a personal relationship with this man. He speaks very fondly of him as a good friend and good man. In his words to Gaius, we find traits that should be true of every follower of Christ as well as every church.

Grounded in Love

Our relationships should be grounded in love. Love for the *"brothers and sisters"* within the church should be a constant. As followers of Jesus, we should be known for this. Not for anger and judgment that is so central to so many congregations. Our love for all people is what should shine through. We should not feel awkward about loving one another. Even though we may not fully agree with the doctrine of every church or group, love should abound over all disagreements when we share the blood of Jesus and the presence of the Holy Spirit. *"Above all, love each other deeply, because love covers over a multitude of sins"* (1 Peter 4:8). Our love for one another could actually overwhelm our anger or lack of trust. The church down the road is not my competition; the folks in that church are my companions on this journey toward righteousness and godliness. I should have a love for them that causes me to desire what is best for them.

Praying for Good

We should be praying for one another, and I don't mean bad prayers. In one country song I have heard, the singer tells of going to church and hearing the preacher insist that Christians must pray for those who have hurt them. Since his girlfriend just left him brokenhearted, he decides that he should actually pray for her. Here are the lyrics:

Pray For You
I pray your brakes go out runnin' down a hill
I pray a flowerpot falls from a window sill
   and knocks you in the head like I'd like to
I pray your birthday comes and nobody calls
I pray you're flyin' high when your engine stalls
I pray all your dreams never come true
Just know wherever you are honey, I pray for you

Now obviously this is not how we should be praying for each other! In fact, if that is your payer habit, keep me out of your prayers! Instead, we should be praying like the Apostle John. He prays for the health and well-being of his friend. That is how we should be praying for all of our *"brothers and sisters"* in Christ.

Bringing Joy

The Apostle also finds great joy in his friend's faith and faithfulness. We really should find joy in one another. I have pastored for a long time now. Unfortunately, I can tell you that not all Christians take joy in the health and well-being of one another. I once was taking a fellow pastor on a tour of the church property and showing him all that God had allowed us to do there. Yes, our property is large, but compared to some it is not as large or impressive. This pastor had faithfully shepherded a smaller church in our community for many years. He had taken care of those folks and was doing a fine job. As we entered the sanctuary, he said something that broke my heart: "Seeing all of this makes a guy like me just want to quit." I was devastated. Had I known he would have that reaction, I would never have shown him around. The last thing I ever want to do is discourage a fellow pastor. I looked at him and said: "Don't think that way. We are all on the same team. And you can win people to Jesus that would never dare enter this church or listen to a word I have to say. You can reach people I can't. And you must keep reaching them!" I don't know if my words helped his perspective or not, but I can tell you I prayed for him that day, and numerous time since. I often pray that God would bless and fill every church. You know, that really is the goal. Every church filled with every person so that every soul knows forgiveness for every sin. Pray for good in the lives of all those who are taking this journey with us.

Serving Faithfully

Gaius has been a faithful servant to the church. Just like the woman in 2 John, Gaius had been housing the traveling teachers and pastors that the Apostles had been sending out, and he had taken good care of them. I think it's wise that the Apostle balanced these two lessons. Be careful whom you welcome into your home so that you are not housing ideas and theologies that will cause damage. Also, be careful to show love and grace to those who come into your care as they are trying to serve our Savior.

Years ago, I was talking to a pastor friend who was between appointments. In order to make a living until his next job, he had started taking speaking engagements anywhere he could get them. The deal was simple; he would preach and the church would take up a love offering (a special offering taken up after the sermon that went to the visiting preacher). I asked him how it was going and he responded with: "Well, there just isn't much love in love offerings! But God is taking care of us." I'm afraid he is right. Sometimes we fail to take proper care of those whom God has sent to speak His word and His will. This is part of Christian faithfulness. Whenever God sends someone to minister the Gospel to us, we should take good care of him or her. I have tried to practice this at every turn in my time as a pastor. Recently, at our church, a group came through from one of our colleges. Now the church took care of their financial needs as part of our budget, and we took good care of them. I was thrilled to hear the college kids tell me that some members of the congregation took their own initiative and bought gift cards to a fast-food place for all the students. Now that is love in action. And to that, the Apostle John would say: *"Dear friend, you are faithful in what you are doing for the brothers and sisters, even though they are strangers to you."*

Day 5

"I wrote to the church, but Diotrephes, who loves to be first, will not welcome us. So when I come, I will call attention to what he is doing, spreading malicious nonsense about us. Not satisfied with that, he even refuses to welcome other believers. He also stops those who want to do so and puts them out of the church. Dear friend, do not imitate what is evil but what is good. Anyone who does what is good is from God. Anyone who does what is evil has not seen God." (3 John 1:9-11)

We have seen an example in Gaius of how the church should act. Now we are introduced to Diotrephes. Here is a man we should not emulate. It seems that the Apostle has written a letter to a church that Diotrephes leads. He may be the pastor or lay leader of this local church, or he may be some type of bishop over a group of churches in the area. Whatever his role, he opposes the work of the Apostle John. Likely he is a part of a group that the Apostle Paul writes to constantly called "Judaizers." These folks did not want the Gentiles (non-Jewish people) to be part of the Church. They felt that Christianity was simply another part of Judaism, and therefore they did not want people trying to bring Gentiles into the Church. Likely Diotrephes is resisting the teachers who have come from John. I don't think I need to point out the level of arrogance it would take to oppose an Apostle this way. One commentary puts it this way about Diotrephes:

Is the type of all vain, noisy, self-asserting teachers, whose main object is to get their own way—an object which they effect by browbeating all who differ from them. No authority is respected and no character spared which seems to oppose their policy. Even an apostle is denounced if he ventures to maintain that the truth may be larger than their view of it. (Spence and Exell 1950, p. 2)

That perfectly captures the problem. In the mind of people like this, the only possible truth is the truth that they have spoken and understood.

That really is arrogant.

No one is smart enough to understand everything, not even within the specific discipline of theology. I have met some folks who think they have it all figured out. They boldly proclaim this truth or that one and boldly oppose anyone who might think differently than them. They arrogantly demand that everyone else follow the Bible the way they do. They dismiss even the possibility that anyone else could have a valid thought, viewpoint, or opinion.

Once when I was a young pastor, I walked out and met the pastor of the church next door. I do mean next door. We stood and talked for a while, so I decided I should invite him to the pastor's prayer group I was attending. He asked me which pastors would be there. I was attending a group that included pastors of Baptists, Pentecostals, Methodists, Church of Christ, and Church of God. When he heard the list, he curled up his lip and said: "Oh no! I couldn't pray with those pastors! They have wrong views of scripture, so I couldn't agree in prayer with them! But if you guys ever get together for golf, I would love to join you." Well, I assure you that I went to my prayer group and we prayed to our Savior Jesus Christ ... and when we went golfing, I did not invite the pastor next door! If he can't pray with us, why should he play with us?

I am being a bit lighthearted about the situation, but actually this is a very sad reality in today's church. We somehow ignore it or just pass it off as normal. The Apostle Paul also warns us when he says, *"Warn them before God against quarreling about words; it is of no value, and only ruins those who listen"* (2 Timothy 2:14). People, like Diotrephes or the pastor next door, are so busy attempting to impose their view of holy living, biblical understanding, or doctrinal purity on others that they miss the call to love. Don't get me wrong. We are clearly called to maintain right doctrine and protect godly practices, but we are called to do all of that in love and understanding. Certainly not out of arrogance and intimidation. In today's culture, that kind of arrogance and intimidation is wrongly seen as leadership and passion. All too often, people flock to someone who arrogantly denounces everyone around them. I suppose it gives them a feeling of being a winner or just being confident. In reality, the leader will use and abuse you just like he has everyone else. Don't follow that person! *"Dear friend, do not imitate what is evil but what is good."*

And we do have an example of what is good.

Our example is Jesus Christ. He really did know it all, but He did not browbeat anyone into following Him. He taught people truth and drew them into acceptance of what He was teaching through a clear show of love by what He was doing. He healed, He touched, He served, He comforted, and He forgave. I just cannot see how arrogance and anger serves Him or serves to further His Kingdom. So let's avoid it, or, quite honestly, God *"will call attention"* to what we are doing. That kind of attention from God will not be very positive.

Day 6

"Demetrius is well spoken of by everyone—and even by the truth itself. We also speak well of him, and you know that our testimony is true." (3 John 1:12)

Oh that this could be said of all of us! In fact, this should be our goal. We should strive to be *"well spoken of by everyone."* We all know someone like this. We all know someone whom everyone likes. The descriptions of such people are pretty uniform. These folks always are honest, helpful, cheerful, and never have a bad word to say about anyone else. They are Christ-like. I have to be honest here and say that I do not believe I would be *"well spoken of by everyone."* I have had too many bad moments in my past to fall into that category, but I still have some time left to fix all of that.

I often speak of my grandfathers. They were both pastors and both served many years in the ministry influencing many lives. I will always remember standing in the funeral line at both funerals. As people would pass by, they would tell me stories. I would hear stories of kindness, direction, healing, and hope. I would hear stories of how my grandfather, their pastor, had changed their lives. And the stories were all different. This description of Demetrius would fit my Grandpa Freeman. He was, in my experience, always kind, gentle, generous, and loving. He was just a wonderful man. As people came through the line at his funeral, they had tears in their eyes as they spoke of him. They were speaking of experiences with their pastor 20-40 years earlier. I was amazed. While I know that I will never be quite that good, I can certainly try and be better each day.

The lesson here is simple to say and difficult to live out.

Be Good to Everyone

Somehow Demetrius is able to show kindness and goodness to everyone he meets. I do believe that some people are just that good. Like Grandpa Freeman, they are gentle and loving, almost by nature, and everyone likes them. However, many of you are less like Grandpa Freeman and more like me. I try to be good to everyone. I try to always be honest, kind, and loving, but sometimes I am not that good at it. Sometimes I just mess up without even realizing it. Other times, I lose my temper and mess up, well, on purpose. But I have noticed something. The longer I walk with Christ, the less I lose my temper and mess up on purpose. So here is my challenge to you, and me. Let's choose to be *"well spoken of by everyone."* When we mess up in that challenge, let's choose to go and ask for forgiveness. Then let's re-engage the challenge and work at being good to everyone.

Be Faithful to the End

Now this challenge will be a long-term endeavor. It is neither a sprint nor a single event. It is a marathon process. We will need to take this thing one day at a time. We will need to wake up every day and say, "Today I am going to be good to everyone to the greatest extent I possibly can." Then we set our minds to live out that promise. When we run headlong into a day where it just doesn't work out and we prove, yet again, that we aren't that good, we ask for forgiveness and start anew the next day. If we practice this process of choosing day after day, then over time it will become part of our normal daily habit. We will be changed slowly, but changed fundamentally. Eventually, we will be *"well spoken of by everyone,"* rather than saying, "well some people like me."

Leave a Great Story

Sometimes when I speak of my grandfathers, I will have people come up to me and say: "You know you are very lucky. I didn't have good role models like that." Sadly, I realize this is true for many people. But the question today is not how good your past relatives were. Although that helps, it isn't the final answer. Our goal in waking up every morning and making the choice to be good to everyone is the making of a great story. Listen, once you are dead and gone, you are in Heaven with Jesus. You no longer have any concerns or worries, but what you leave behind is a story. Your kids, your family, your grandkids, and your friends will talk about you. They will remember you. They will tell stories about you. And you get to write the story that they will tell. Don't miss this truth. Every day, you are writing the story of your life. In the end, you will not be the one telling it, but it will be told. What will it sound like?

He was a great guy ... but ...

She meant well ... but ...

Or it could be ... He was *"well spoken of by everyone."*

The choice is yours.

Day 7

"I have much to write you, but I do not want to do so with pen and ink. I hope to see you soon, and we will talk face to face. Peace to you. The friends here send their greetings. Greet the friends there by name." (3 John 1:13-14)

There is always so much to say. No single letter can say it all. No single book can capture it all. No single conversation can encompass all that we want or need to say and learn. It takes a lifetime, and even then we will feel like we have left something out. The Apostle John has just that feeling here as he wraps up his letter to Gaius. Just as he wrote when wrapping up the letter to the lady in 2 John, he points out that he has more to say. Wouldn't you love to somehow have a video of his conversation with Gaius when they finally got together? Wouldn't you love to know the things that the Apostle John wanted to tell his friend?

Many scholars think that these three letters were written late in the Apostle John's life. Perhaps even written after he had written his Gospel and his Revelation. If that is true, then this question becomes all the more intriguing. What more would he want to say? He has said so much already, yet there is always more to say. As he pens these letters, assuming he is at the end of his life and maybe 80-90 years old, his mind likely races with all of the other things he should say. All of the advice he would still like to give. All of the truth that he wants to make sure gets taught and properly learned and applied. That kind of teaching comes across best when it's face-to-face, so he waits for the opportunity to speak in person.

Today, we have a habit of simply "tagging" people with information. Then we believe that we have somehow taught when oftentimes we have failed to teach or properly communicate. We send an email or text a picture or emoji and feel satisfied that we have communicated. We actually have not touched someone's life. I know some are going to disagree here, but you just cannot replace being in person. So much more is communicated, so much more is taught, and so much more is caught when we speak face-to-face. I once heard a leadership guru say, "More is caught than is taught." This is absolutely true. My children did not do what I told them to do; instead, they did what they saw me do. They caught some things from me that I never taught them. Most of the things they caught were good, but some were not so good. Good, bad, or indifferent ... they caught it. This is true in your spiritual life. As you follow Christ and try to teach others to do the same, you need to realize that the best teacher is time spent with the person. The time I spent with a leader is far more valuable than the time I spent listening to a leader. The time I spent with a teacher is far more valuable than the time I spent listening to a teacher. The time I spent with a friend is far more important to me than the time I spent on the phone with a friend. Now, I listen and take notes when I am with teachers and leaders, but it's in watching their facial expressions, body language, intensity, compassion, and passion that I actually learn some of the greatest lessons. It's catching in-person what you could never see on paper that makes all the difference. I actually believe that the best way to learn is face-to-face. I love learning. Not real fond of school, but I love learning most from someone who is passionate about what is being taught. I have taken many classes over my lifetime, and most recently I have taken online classes. Although I have learned from every one of those online classes, it just isn't the same. An email doesn't convey the same passion or energy. A message on the student platform is not the same as a conversation in the classroom or in the coffee shop. Learning is so much better in person. So the Apostle waits for the opportunity to say all he desires to say ... in person.

Then he leaves behind peace. Again, what if we could all do that? Leave peace in our wake. What if we left peace in the hearts of everyone we met? Perhaps that is the overarching lesson of all three letters, the Gospel of John, and even the Revelation of St. John. What if the real goal of all that work and words was so that the believer in Christ could find peace? Maybe all those words were meant to give us peace.

Peace because we know God's word (1 John 1:1-4).

Peace because we are walking in the light (1 John 1:5-7).

Peace because we are avoiding sin (1 John 2:1-14).

Peace because we are protecting our hearts from this world and from antichrists (1 John 2:15-26).

Peace because we know we are children of God (1 John 2:28, 3:10).

Peace because we live out love (1 John 3:11-24).

Peace because we follow the true Spirit of God (1 John 4:1-6).

Peace because we know God's love (1 John 4:7-21).

Peace because we have faith in the Son of God, Jesus (1 John 5).

Peace because we protect against false teachers (2 John).

Peace because we are learning to be *"well spoken of by everyone"* (3 John).

Let's end the way so many of the Epistles begin:

"Grace, mercy and peace from God the Father and from Jesus Christ, the Father's Son, will be with us in truth and love." (2 John 1:3)

REFERENCES

Spence, H. D. M. and Joseph S. Exell. 1950. *The Pulpit Commentary*. Grand Rapids, Michigan: Wm. B. Eerdmans Publishing Company.

McGee, J. Vernon. 1983. *Thru The Bible*. Nashville, Tennessee: Thomas Nelson Publishers.

Strong, James. 2010. *The New Strong's Expanded Exhaustive Concordance of the Bible*. Nashville, Tennessee: Thomas Nelson Publishers.

Architects of Peace Foundation. Elie Wiesel Biography. http://www.architectsofpeace.org/architects-of-peace/elie-wiesel.

Blue Letter Bible. 2016. blueletterbible.org. https://www.blueletterbible.org/niv/1jo/1/1/s_1160001

All scripture quotations, unless otherwise noted, are taken from the Holy Bible, New International Version.

ABOUT THE AUTHOR

Mike Hilson is the Senior Pastor of New Life Church. Starting out in 1999 in La Plata, Maryland, with a congregation of less than 100 attendees, New Life Church has grown tremendously multiplying into several churches and video venues with now more than 5,000 in regular attendance. In addition, New Life Church has a significant presence in local and international relief work. Mike also currently serves on the Board of Trustees at Southern Wesleyan University. He lives in La Plata with his wife, Tina. They have three sons, Robert, Stephen, and Joshua, who have taken this journey of ministry with them.

Other books by Mike Hilson include *Napkin Theology, Speak Life, A Significant Impact for Christ, Coffee with the Pastor — the book of James,* and *Coffee with the Pastor — The Chase: King David's Pursuit of the Heart of God.*